Arts & Crafts for Home Decorating®

BEDROOM DECORATING

D0521411

The Home Decorating Institute™

Copyright © 1991 Cy DeCosse Incorporated 5900 Green Oak Drive Minnetonka, Minnesota 55343
1-800-328-3895 All rights reserved Printed in U.S.A.

Library of Congress Cataloging-in-Publication Data Bedroom Decorating. p. cm. — (Arts & crafts for home decorating)
Includes index. ISBN 0-86573-350-3 ISBN 0-86573-351-1 (pbk.)   1. Bedrooms. 2. Interior decoration. I. Cy DeCosse
Incorporated. II. Series.   NK2117.B4B424 1991 747.7'7—dc20   91-807

CONTENTS

Selecting a Style

Beds & Bedding

Window Treatments

Creative
Storage Ideas

Finishing
Touches

SELECTING A STYLE

Keep your individual needs in mind when choosing the style and furnishings for your bedroom. For many, the bedroom is more than a place to sleep and change clothes. Ideally, it offers privacy and serves as a place for a quiet retreat from activity. Often the bedroom doubles as a sewing room or a study.

There are three general styles of decorating: traditional, contemporary, and transitional. Depending on the one you prefer, furnishings range from detailed and elaborate to streamlined and simple.

The fabrics and other materials you select can help carry out the decorating style. For example, a mix of patterns and colors works well in traditional bedrooms, while fewer colors and patterns are often associated with contemporary decors.

When deciding on the style for your bedroom, consider whether you want the room to be formal or informal. Textured surfaces and matte finishes give an informal feeling to a room, while smooth surfaces are generally more formal. Some fabrics have contemporary patterns, such as abstract designs, while others may have traditional patterns, such as cabbage roses, that are associated with certain period styles.

Add interest to the bedroom by varying the textures of the fabrics and other materials. If the bedroom is predominantly one color, it is especially important to vary the textures. A smooth, crisp chintz fabric can be combined with a linen or novelty weave. Keep in mind that walls, floors, and room accessories have textures. A smooth brass headboard can contrast with a tapestry bedspread. Shiny hardwood flooring can contrast with a plush area rug.

Color is a key element in a bedroom's decor. When selecting a color scheme for your bedroom, it is more important to be guided by your own personal favorites than to be swayed by current trends. Light colors tend to make a space appear larger than it really is. For this reason, ceilings are often painted white, visually raising them for a more expansive feeling. A high ceiling or walls in a large bedroom, however, can be painted a darker color to make the bedroom look smaller and more cozy.

Use the following pages as a guide to develop the decor for your bedroom, incorporating your own personal tastes, rather than following any one style. Remember, your bedroom is an important room in your home, so plan a style that you will be comfortable with.

TRADITIONAL STYLE

Lavish and detailed, traditional bedrooms feature rich woods and patterned fabrics in distinctive colors.

In decorating, "traditional" encompasses a wide range of period styles. Traditional bedrooms are cozy and comfortable, often featuring a mix of patterns on walls, windows, and beds.

Rich in detail, traditional bedrooms are lavishly decorated with fabrics, from elaborate tapestries to cotton chintz or sateen. Long draperies may puddle luxuriously onto the floor. The bed is often dressed with layers of bedspreads and bed skirts, and the linens may be embroidered or lace-trimmed. Furniture of rich woods, such as mahogany or cherry, is frequently used in traditional rooms.

A traditional bedroom can be the perfect place to express your own personal taste. Favorite antiques, family photographs, and collections of personal memorabilia are often displayed in traditional bedrooms.

ELEMENTS OF A TRADITIONAL BEDROOM

Furniture of rich, dark wood *is intricately detailed. The brass lamps carry out the traditional theme on bedside tables.*

Bishop sleeve curtains *(page 80) are billowy and opulent. In keeping with the lavish traditional style, the fabric is generously puddled onto the floor and the curtains are held in place with tiebacks. A gathered rod-pocket valance (page 78) borders the window at the upper edge.*

Ruffled pillow shams *(page 48) can repeat the detailing of a ruffled bedspread.*

Four-poster mahogany bed is covered with a short ruffled bedspread (page 33) over a gathered skirt (page 52). Several patterned fabrics in a mixture of distinctive colors are used for accent pillows on the bed.

Fabric border along the ceiling is cut from coordinating fabric and carries the floral pattern throughout the room. Fabric-covered boxes (page 89) and other accessories complete the traditional look.

ACCESSORIES FOR A TRADITIONAL BEDROOM

Picture frame *displays a favorite heirloom or offers protection for a valued antique.*

Writing desk *lends a homey; old-fashioned look to the traditional bedroom. A collection of small boxes holds desk supplies.*

Wastebasket, *covered with a traditional tapestry fabric, coordinates with the room decor.*

Porcelain flowers *(page 124) embellish a picture frame.*

Bedside steps, *made from mahogany, stand next to a high traditional bed.*

Bandboxes *(page 94), originally made to store men's collar bands, are used today for decorative as well as for practical purposes.*

CONTEMPORARY STYLE

Contemporary decorating can be described as "less is more," with the number of furnishings and accessories kept to a minimum.

This approach to decorating, which makes rooms look more spacious, requires the careful selection of each element. In many contemporary rooms, an outstanding piece of furniture, a dramatic floor covering, or a high-style painting becomes a focal point, with otherwise streamlined furnishings as the backdrop. Many elements have angular, crisp design lines, but angular edges may be rounded off for a softer, more comfortable look.

Color is often kept to a minimum. To emphasize the spacious look, light cool colors are often used, except in large rooms. Neutrals are also frequently used.

Bare or nearly bare walls may be painted in a solid color or, for subtle interest, they can be sponged in muted tones. Berber carpeting, dhurrie rugs, or highly polished hardwood floors work well in a contemporary bedroom. Window treatments are chosen to offer privacy, but are never complicated or fussy. For simplicity in styling, tailored blinds or pleated shades are good choices.

Dramatic lighting adds to the refined look of contemporary styling. Recessed lighting, cove lighting, and ceiling-mounted track lighting are frequently used. For a floating effect, fluorescent tubes can be installed under the platform of a platform bed.

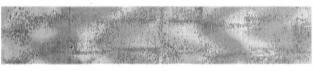

ELEMENTS OF A
CONTEMPORARY BEDROOM

Table lamps *of brass or chrome with sleek design lines are suitable for contemporary bedrooms. The polished metals add richness to the decor.*

Lacquered furniture *has a slick, polished appearance. For simple design, contemporary end tables and dressers often do not have drawer pulls.*

Knife-edge pillows, *generous in size and free from detailing, show off the fabrics and add softness.*

Faux finishes *(page 111) add subtle texture to otherwise plain surfaces, as in the clock (above) and vase (below).*

The window treatment features a stylish rounded-rod cornice (page 84). The tailored, pleated shades complete the no-fuss, contemporary look.

The bed and bedding have a softly padded yet streamlined look. The channel quilting of the fitted bedspread (page 34) emphasizes the straight lines of the bed surround (page 60). The padded headboard (page 64) has a rounded border, framing the head of the bed.

ACCESSORIES FOR A CONTEMPORARY BEDROOM

Illuminated glass-block bookends *are a nice addition to otherwise dark bookshelves. Cut a wood base to fit the opening of a glass block vase, and mount a small light bulb on the base.*

A pedestal *is a stately accessory that provides a base for contemporary artwork or a plant. Pedestals may be sprayed with a textural granite finish, decoratively painted, or covered with fabric.*

Wastebaskets *can be covered with contemporary fabric to coordinate with any bedroom decor.*

Glass shelves *provide a sleek display unit for contemporary collections and small objects. Simple metal bookends turned upside down serve as brackets.*

Picture frames *for contemporary rooms can be crafted from simple materials. This frame is made from two wooden dowels; a flat, thin board; and two pieces of clear plastic.*

Hand-painted chair *(page 118) is an exciting contemporary art piece. Unpainted-furniture stores and garage sales are good places to find inexpensive furniture for this kind of project.*

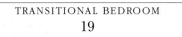

TRANSITIONAL STYLE

Transitional, or "eclectic," style combines the best qualities of traditional and contemporary.

Transitional decorating integrates elements from several styles, providing the warmth of traditional with the simplicity of contemporary. Exciting and more personal decors are often achieved by blending styles, rather than slavishly following one theme.

In transitional rooms, a mix of contemporary and traditional furniture can offer an effective contrast. For a balanced look, the pieces of furniture should appear similar in weight or proportion. Often, contemporary pieces of furniture are inspired by familiar traditional styles, making them especially suitable for transitional decorating. The bed, for example, has some of the detailing seen in traditional furniture, but the glossy, white paint and the smooth lines give it a crisp, contemporary look.

Color can unify varied styles of furnishings so they work together. Repeat only a few of the colors and fabrics in the room, and avoid mixing several patterns.

ELEMENTS OF A
TRANSITIONAL BEDROOM

The bedding ensemble *is a mix of styles. The ruffled pillow shams (page 48), traditional in styling, are paired with a buttoned duvet cover (page 45) for a more updated look. Additional pillows with flanges (page 49) complete* the eclectic mix. A unified color selection blends the bedding fabrics, from contemporary pinstripes to traditional floral chintz.

A traditional-style armoire *(opposite) mixes well with contemporary furnishings, provided the pieces in the room are similar in weight or proportion.*

Classic curtains *(opposite) are shown with a contemporary drapery pole. The leaded glass window provides added drama.*

Nightstands *(opposite) in transitional bedrooms can contrast effectively with the accessories. A traditionally styled nightstand can set off a contemporary lamp and picture, or a contemporary nightstand can provide a base for an old-fashioned dried flower arrangement.*

Baskets *are versatile and blend with many decorating styles, adding warmth to a room.*

ACCESSORIES FOR A
TRANSITIONAL BEDROOM

Vanity mirror is embellished with a fabric bow to coordinate with other room accessories. Use craft fabric stiffener to give the bow extra body for shaping.

Quilt ladder is a unique way to store and display quilts.

Small storage chest for personal keepsakes is dyed, or pickled, with colored stain (page 120).

Headboard is creatively painted (page 118) for a personalized, whimsical effect.

Handmade shelves provide a base for displaying artistic candles.

Sisal mats, dyed, or pickled, with colored stains (page 120), add texture to a room. They may be used as floor mats or wall hangings.

Beds & Bedding

BEDDING BASICS

Make your own bedspreads, coverlets, duvet covers, bed skirts, and pillow shams to fit the decor of your bedroom. Decorator fabrics such as chintzes and sateens are good choices for bedding, because they are durable and drape well. Sheets may also be used; their width makes seaming unnecessary on some projects.

Whether the bed is a twin, full, queen, or king, the measurements will vary within each category, depending on the model or manufacturer. Measure the bed to make custom bed coverings and bed skirts that fit perfectly. Take the measurements over the blankets and sheets that will normally be used on the bed, to ensure that the bed covering will fit correctly. Measure the length of the bed from the head of the bed to the foot **(a),** and the width of the bed from side to side **(b).**

Duvets and coverlets reach 1" to 4" (2.5 to 10 cm) below the mattress on the sides and at the foot of the bed. Determine the drop length of the duvet or coverlet by measuring the distance from the top of the bed to the desired position for the lower edge of the duvet or coverlet **(c).** The drop length is usually 9" to 12" (23 to 30.5 cm), depending on the mattress depth.

When measuring for a full-length bedspread, measure the drop length from the top of the mattress to the floor; then subtract ½" (1.3 cm) for clearance **(d).**

When measuring for a bed skirt, measure the drop length from the top of the box spring to the floor **(e);** then subtract ½" (1.3 cm) for clearance.

Bed pillows also vary in size, depending on the amount of stuffing used. For best results, measure the bed pillow to determine the size of the pillow sham.

Measure the bed rather than rely on standardized bed measurements.

Determine the finished size of a pillow sham by measuring around the pillow, in length **(a)** and width **(b),** and dividing these measurements by two.

BEDSPREADS

The basic bedspread, unlined and hemmed on all sides, is the easiest bed covering to make. A full-length bedspread looks best when made from heavier fabric that drapes well, such as a damask or tapestry. A shorter, comforter-length bedspread, or coverlet, which is used with a bed skirt, can be made from a fabric that is lighter in weight. To embellish bedspreads, use trims such as fringe or lace to finish the edges (pages 30 and 31).

HOW TO MAKE A BASIC BEDSPREAD

CUTTING DIRECTIONS

Determine the drop length for the bedspread (page 27). Determine the finished length of the bedspread by measuring the length of the mattress from the head of the bed to the foot; then add the desired drop length for the foot of the bed. If you want the bedspread to cover the bed pillows, add an extra 15" to 20" (38 to 51 cm) to tuck under and wrap around the pillows. The cut length of the bedspread is equal to the finished length plus 3" (7.5 cm) for hem allowances.

Determine the finished width of the bedspread by measuring the width of the mattress from side to side, then adding two drop lengths. Cut one full width of fabric for a center panel and two equal, partial widths for side panels; the panels are seamed together to make the bedspread. The cut width of the bedspread, after the panels are pieced together, is the finished width plus 1" (2.5 cm) for hem allowances.

To calculate how many widths of fabric are needed, divide the cut width of the bedspread by the fabric width; round off to the next highest number. Multiply the number of widths by the cut length of the bedspread for the amount of fabric needed.

1 Seam center and side panels, right sides together. Finish seam allowances by serging or zigzagging; press. Press under ½" (1.3 cm) along upper edge of bedspread; then press under 2" (5 cm).

2 Place the bedspread on the bed with equal drop length distributed on sides and foot of bed. Pin-mark one corner of bedspread along edge of mattress at foot of bed.

3 Fold the bedspread in half lengthwise; place on flat surface. Measure from pin marks in step 2 to desired finished length plus ½" (1.3 cm) hem allowance, at 2" to 3" (5 to 7.5 cm) intervals; mark with chalk. Cut through both layers of fabric to round lower corners.

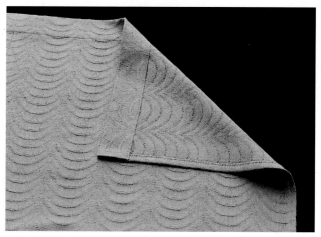

4 Finish side and lower edges. Press under ½" (1.3 cm), and topstitch ⅜" (1 cm) from foldline. Stitch hem at upper edge.

IDEAS FOR BEDSPREADS

A variety of looks can be achieved using different trims. Ruffles and lace trims are used for a romantic decor, fabric-covered welting for a casual, tailored look, and twisted welting or fringe for more elegance. The upper edge of the bedspread is hemmed, and the lower and side edges are finished with trim.

Twisted welting *(page 32) is added to a bedspread for a look that is tailored and elegant.*

Stuffed ruffles *(page 33) give a more casual and whimsical look.*

Double-knotted fringe *(page 33) is elegantly traditional when used on a bedspread made from tapestry fabric.*

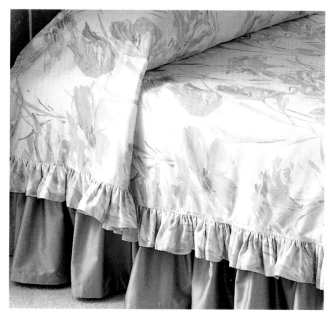

Ruffles (page 33) are added to a bedspread for a traditional, romantic style.

Fabric-covered welting (page 32) is added to a bedspread for a crisp look. The bedspread may also feature welting at the seams (page 44).

Lace edging (page 33) is romantic and luxurious. Lace has also been topstitched over the seams on the bedspread for an added embellishment.

HOW TO MAKE A BEDSPREAD WITH TWISTED WELTING

CUTTING DIRECTIONS

Determine size of bedspread and cut the panels as for basic bedspread on page 29, subtracting the finished width of trim from cut length and two times the finished width of trim from cut width. Cut twisted welting to a length equal to the distance around sides and lower edge plus 2" (5 cm).

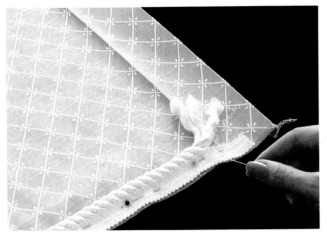

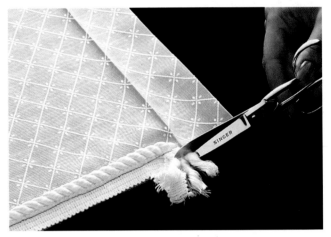

1 Follow steps 1 to 3 on page 29. Finish side and lower edges. Pin twisted welting to right side of bedspread with welt ½" (1.3 cm) from raw edge and with ends extending 1" (2.5 cm) beyond hemline. Remove stitching from welting tape for about 1½" (3.8 cm) at ends. Untwist end of welting.

2 Curve welting into seam allowance; pin. Stitch welting to bedspread, ½" (1.3 cm) from raw edge, using zipper foot. Trim ends of welting. Press seam allowances toward bedspread; finish as in step 2, opposite, for bedspread with ruffle.

HOW TO MAKE A BEDSPREAD WITH FABRIC WELTING

CUTTING DIRECTIONS

Determine size of bedspread and cut the panels as for basic bedspread on page 29, subtracting the finished width of trim from cut length and two times the finished width of trim from cut width. Cut bias welting strips to a length equal to distance around sides and lower edge of bedspread plus extra for piecing (page 44).

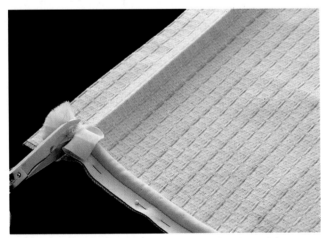

1 Follow steps 1 to 3 on page 29. Finish side and lower edges. Make welting as in steps 1 and 2 on page 44; pin to right side of bedspread, matching raw edges and with ends of welting extending 1" (2.5 cm) beyond hemline. Remove stitching from welting for 1" (2.5 cm) at ends; remove cording up to hemline.

2 Curve welting into seam allowance; pin. Stitch welting to bedspread, using zipper foot. Trim ends of welting. Press seam allowances toward bedspread; finish as in step 2, opposite, for bedspread with ruffle.

HOW TO MAKE A BEDSPREAD WITH A RUFFLE

CUTTING DIRECTIONS

Determine size of bedspread and cut the panels as for basic bedspread on page 29, subtracting the finished width of trim from cut length and two times the finished width of trim from cut width. For ruffle, cut fabric strips as on page 42; or for stuffed ruffle, cut fabric strips and polyester upholstery batting as on page 43.

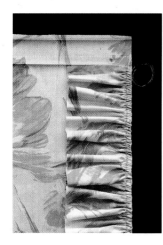

1 Follow steps 1 to 3 on page 29. Make ruffle and apply it, with ends of ruffle at hemline, as in steps 1 to 3 on page 42. Or make stuffed ruffle and apply it, with ends of ruffle at hemline, as in steps 1 to 3 on page 43. Finish seam allowances by zigzagging or serging; press toward bedspread.

2 Stitch hem in place at upper edge. Topstitch along sides and lower edge from right side ⅜" (1 cm) from seam, stitching through seam allowances. Machine-stitch or hand-stitch ends of hem.

HOW TO MAKE A BEDSPREAD WITH FRINGE OR LACE

CUTTING DIRECTIONS

Determine size of bedspread and cut the panels as for basic bedspread on page 29, subtracting the finished width of trim from cut length and two times the finished width of trim from cut width. Cut fringe or lace trim to a length equal to the distance around sides and lower edge plus 2" (5 cm).

1 Follow steps 1 to 3 on page 29. Finish side and lower edges. Stitch hem at upper edge; pin trim on bedspread, right sides up, with end of trim extending 1" (2.5 cm) beyond hemmed edge and with upper edge of trim ½" (1.3 cm) from edge of bedspread. Pin in place up to curve of corner.

2 Ease the trim around rounded corner; steam to shape trim. If necessary, hand-stitch a row of gathering stitches through the heading of the trim to distribute fullness. Continue to pin trim to bedspread on the lower edge and remaining side, shaping the trim at remaining corner.

3 Stitch along inner edge of trim, using straight stitch or narrow zigzag stitch. Remove gathering stitches.

4 Fold ends of trim under twice to wrong side of bedspread, making ½" (1.3 cm) double-fold hem; stitch. For sheer lace, seam allowance may be pressed toward bedspread and edgestitched before finishing ends.

FITTED BEDSPREADS

For a contemporary look, a fitted bedspread with channel quilting can be used on a bed with a bed surround (page 60) or on a platform bed. The bedspread fits over the mattress like a fitted sheet and has elastic at the corners to hold it in place. The channels may vary in width, but should not be wider than 10" (25.5 cm). For variety, choose two or three fabrics for the channels. Because the bedspread is fitted, the measurements should be taken over the blankets you intend to use on the bed.

HOW TO MAKE A FITTED BEDSPREAD

MATERIALS

- Decorator fabric in one or more colors.
- Polyester upholstery batting, 54" (137 cm) wide; two cut lengths are needed for twin size, full size, and queen size; three lengths are needed for king size.
- Lightweight lining fabric, such as batiste.
- 1½ yd. (1.4 m) elastic, ¾" (2 cm) wide.

CUTTING DIRECTIONS

Calculate a measurement equal to the width of the mattress plus two times the mattress depth, plus 12" (30.5 cm) for tucking under the mattress, plus 6" (15 cm) for the side hems. Divide this measurement by the number of channels desired to find the finished width of each channel.

Cut the channels on the lengthwise grain of the fabric. The cut width of each channel is equal to the finished width of the channel plus 1" (2.5 cm) for seam allowances plus ¼" (6 mm) to allow for the shrinkage that will occur due to quilting.

The cut length of each channel is equal to the length of the mattress plus the mattress depth plus 6" (15 cm) for tuck-under and 7" (18 cm) for hem allowances.

Determine the number of channels that can be cut from each fabric width by dividing the fabric width by the cut width of each channel; then determine how many fabric widths are needed by dividing the number of channels needed by the number of channels per width, rounding up to the next fabric width.

To calculate the amount of fabric you will need, multiply the number of fabric widths needed by the cut length of the channels. If using more than one fabric, calculate the amount of fabric needed in each color separately. The cut size of the lining and batting is 8" (20.5 cm) wider and longer than the bedspread top will be after the channels are stitched together. Piece the lining and batting as necessary.

1 Stitch the channel strips together on lengthwise edges, using ½" (1.3 cm) seam allowances. Seam lining widths together as necessary.

2 Place lining, right side down, on flat surface. Place first width of batting over lining, along one side.

3 Place bedspread front 4" (10 cm) from outer edges of batting, right side up; secure layers, using pins. Fold back bedspread and pin seam allowances of inner channel to batting and lining, pinning through all layers.

(Continued)

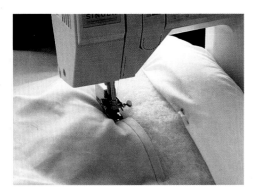

4 Roll up extra batting and lining, and position under arm of sewing machine; hold in place, using pins or bicycle clips. Stitch pinned seam through all layers over previous stitching. Use walking foot, if available.

5 Reposition layers on flat surface. Pin next seam to batting and lining through all layers as in step 3, and stitch as in step 4. Seam will be stitched in the opposite direction from first seam.

6 Continue to pin and stitch seams, working toward side of bedspread, until half of bedspread is quilted. Leave outer edge of bedspread unstitched.

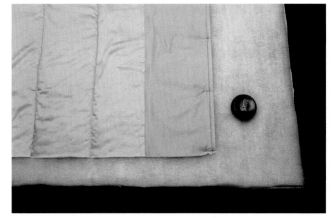

7 Cut through half the thickness of batting 1" to 2" (2.5 to 5 cm) from inner edge; pull layer away. Repeat on one edge of remaining width of batting. Place remaining batting over wrong side of lining, lapping batting layers for even thickness; press together, using hands.

8 Pin and stitch seam of channel at middle of bedspread. Continue to pin and stitch seams on second half, working toward side of bedspread.

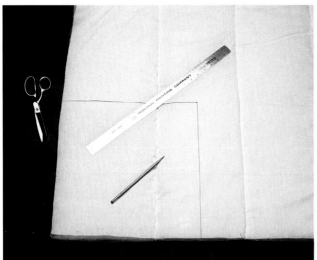

9 Trim batting and lining to same size as bedspread front. Measure from sides and lower edge, on wrong side, an amount equal to depth of mattress plus hem and tuck-in allowance. Mark seamlines for corners at foot of bed.

10 Add 1" (2.5 cm) seam allowances; cut out corners. Finish the seam allowances.

11 Pin finished edges together at corner; stitch, starting at outer edges.

12 Fold bedspread at corner with seam allowances centered as shown. Stitch diagonally across corner to prevent sharp point.

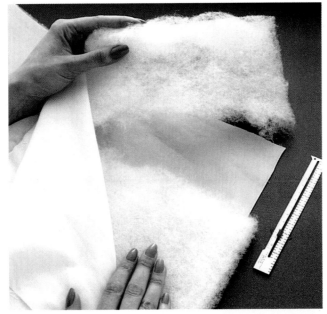

13 Pull away some of the batting in the hem allowances to taper thickness. Hem allowances are 3" (7.5 cm) at sides and lower edge and 4" (10 cm) at upper edge.

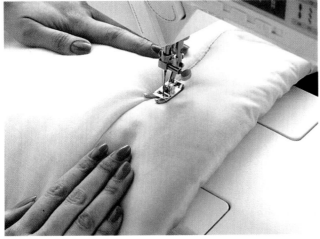

14 Press under ½" (1.3 cm) on upper edge; then press under 3½" (9 cm). Pin hem in place; stitch.

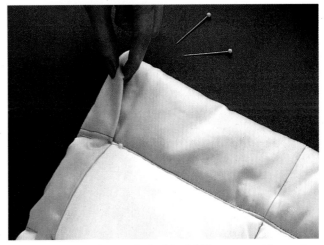

15 Press 1½" (3.8 cm) double-fold hems on sides and lower edge. Pin corners diagonally at upper edge.

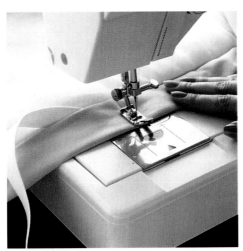

16 Stitch hem on one side, stopping 12" (30.5 cm) from corner at foot of bed. Mark elastic 12" (30.5 cm) from one end; insert in hem, stitching across end.

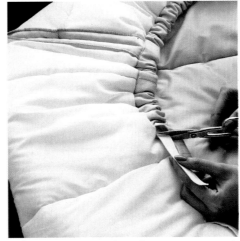

17 Continue stitching hem, encasing elastic; stop 12" (30.5 cm) beyond corner. Pull up elastic to mark. Stitch across end of elastic; cut off excess.

18 Finish hem, repeating steps 16 and 17 for other corner.

DUVET COVERS

HOW TO MAKE A BASIC DUVET COVER

A duvet cover protects a duvet, or comforter, from wear. Although frequently paired with bed skirts (page 50), duvet covers also work well with bed surrounds (page 60). Duvet covers can be edged with welting for a tailored look, or bordered with ruffles for a romantic look.

MATERIALS

• Decorator fabric, sheeting, or batiste.

• Two zippers, each 22" (56 cm) long.

CUTTING DIRECTIONS

Determine the finished size of the duvet cover by measuring the duvet. The finished duvet cover may be the same size as the duvet measurements. Or for a snug fit over a down duvet, the cover may be up to 2" (5 cm) shorter and narrower than the duvet.

To determine how many widths of fabric are needed, divide the width of the duvet cover by the fabric width; round off to the next highest number. Multiply the number of widths by twice the length of the duvet to calculate the amount of fabric needed.

For both the front and back of the duvet cover, cut one full width of fabric for a center panel and two equal, partial widths for side panels; the panels are seamed together to make both the front and back of the duvet cover. The cut size of the front, after seaming, is 1" (2.5 cm) wider and longer than the finished size. Cut the back of the cover the same width as the front, and 1½" (3.8 cm) shorter than the front. Cut a zipper strip 3½" (9 cm) wide and the same length as the cut width of the back.

1 Serge or zigzag upper edge of zipper strip and lower edge of duvet cover back. Press finished edge of the zipper strip under ½" (1.3 cm), and finished edge of the back under 1" (2.5 cm).

2 Place closed zippers face down on seam allowance of the back, with zipper tabs meeting in center and with edge of zipper tapes on fold. Using zipper foot, stitch along one side of zippers.

3 Turn right side up. Place pressed edge of zipper strip along edge of zipper teeth on other side of the zippers, and stitch close to edge. Backstitch at the end of zippers.

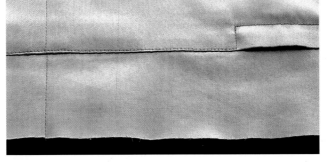

4 Stitch across end of one zipper; topstitch through all layers to stitch seam from zipper to side of cover. Repeat to stitch from other end of zipper to opposite side. Open zippers. Round lower corners, if desired, as on page 29, steps 2 and 3. (Contrasting thread was used to show detail.)

5 Pin duvet cover front to back, right sides together; stitch. Turn right side out.

IDEAS FOR DUVET COVERS

$\bigvee$ary the look of duvet covers by adding ruffles or welting. Follow the basic steps for making duvet covers, inserting the ruffles or welting as on pages 42 to 44. Or add buttons or tucks to the duvet front, following the steps on page 45.

Ruffles (page 42) give a duvet cover a more romantic, feminine look. They are attached only to the sides and lower edge of the cover. On the duvet cover shown, welting has also been added. First apply the welting to the duvet front; then apply the ruffle.

Stuffed ruffles (page 43), an innovative variation of ruffles, border a duvet cover with softness.

Welting (page 44) defines the edges of a duvet cover for a classic look.

Tucked duvet covers (page 45) feature lengthwise tucks on each side. The wide tucks add interest and detailing to the large expanse of fabric.

Buttoned duvet covers (page 45) are charming and practical. Buttonholes on the duvet cover and buttons on the duvet keep these two components neatly in place.

HOW TO MAKE A DUVET COVER WITH A RUFFLE

MATERIALS

- Decorator fabric.
- Two zippers, each 22" (56 cm) long.
- Cord, such as pearl cotton, for gathering.

CUTTING DIRECTIONS

Cut front, back, and zipper strip as on page 39. Cut fabric strips for ruffle on crosswise or lengthwise grain, with combined length of strips two to three times the distance to be ruffled, allowing for double or triple fullness. Ruffles are only attached to the sides and lower edge of a duvet cover. Width of strips is two times the finished width of ruffle plus 1" (2.5 cm) for seam allowances.

1 Stitch fabric strips for ruffle together in ¼" (6 mm) seams, right sides together. Fold pieced strip in half lengthwise, right sides together; stitch across ends in ¼" (6 mm) seams. Turn right side out; press ends and foldline.

2 Zigzag over cord a scant ½" (1.3 cm) from raw edges. For more control when adjusting gathers, zigzag over a second cord, within seam allowance, ¼" (6 mm) from first cord.

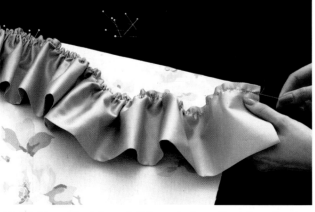

3 Divide ruffle strip and distance to be gathered on duvet cover front into fourths; pin-mark. Place ruffle strip on duvet cover front, right sides together, matching raw edges and pin marks; pull gathering cords to fit. Pin in place; stitch.

4 Follow steps 1 to 4 on page 39. Pin front to back, right sides together. Stitch inside previous stitches. Turn right side out.

HOW TO MAKE A DUVET COVER WITH A STUFFED RUFFLE

MATERIALS

- Decorator fabric.
- Two zippers, each 22" (56 cm) long.
- Upholstery batting.
- Cord, such as pearl cotton, for gathering.

CUTTING DIRECTIONS

Cut front, back, and zipper strip as on page 39. Cut fabric strips for ruffle on crosswise or lengthwise grain, with combined length of strips two times the distance to be ruffled, allowing for double fullness. Ruffles are only attached to the sides and lower edge of a duvet cover. Width of strips is two times finished width of ruffle plus 2" (5 cm). Cut strips of upholstery batting, with combined length of strips equal to finished length of ruffle plus 3" (7.5 cm) for each corner. Width of batting strips is 1½" (3.8 cm) less than finished width of ruffle.

1 Stitch fabric strips for ruffle together in ¼" (6 mm) seams, right sides together. Piece batting strips by butting edges and whipstitching them together by hand.

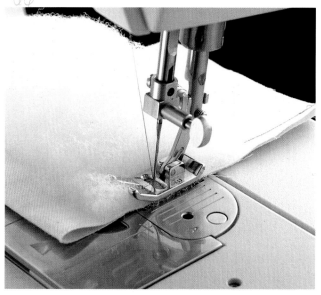

2 Fold ruffle strip in half lengthwise, right sides together; at ends, pin batting strip over ruffle ¾" (2 cm) from fold. Stitch across ends of ruffle, catching batting in stitches; turn right side out.

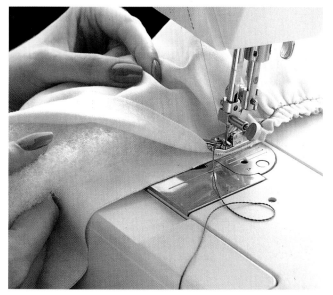

3 Zigzag over cord a scant ½" (1.3 cm) from raw edges, encasing batting; do not catch batting in stitches. Stop at 10" (25.5 cm) intervals, leaving needle down; gently pull up on batting and cord, gathering fabric behind needle. Distribute gathers evenly. Apply ruffle as in step 3, opposite.

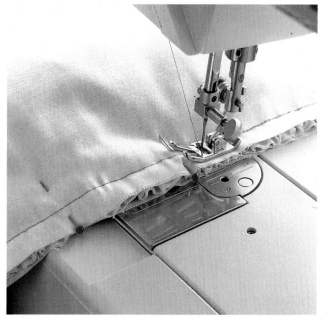

4 Follow steps 1 to 4 on page 39. Pin front to back, right sides together. Stitch inside previous stitches. Turn right side out.

HOW TO MAKE A DUVET COVER WITH WELTING

MATERIALS

- Decorator fabric.
- Two zippers, each 22" (56 cm) long.
- Cording, up to ¾" (2 cm) in diameter.

CUTTING DIRECTIONS

Cut front, back, and zipper strip as on page 39. Cut bias welting strips as in step 1.

not tight to cord – reduces ripping later

1 Pin fabric around cording; measure this distance and add 1" (2.5 cm) for seam allowances. Cut bias welting strips to this width, with combined length of strip equal to distance around duvet cover plus an allowance for seaming and easing.

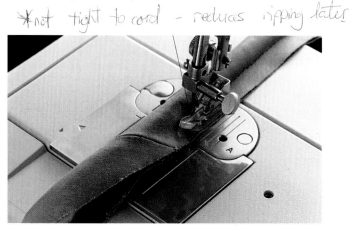

2 Seam fabric strips together. Fold strip around cording, wrong sides together, matching raw edges. Using a zipper foot, machine-baste close to cording.

3 Stitch welting to right side of duvet front over previous stitches, matching raw edges and starting 2" (5 cm) from end of welting; clip and ease welting at corners, or ease at curves.

4 Stop stitching 2" (5 cm) from point where ends of welting will meet. Cut off one end of welting so it overlaps the other end by 1" (2.5 cm).

5 Remove stitching from one end of welting, and trim ends of cording so they just meet.

6 Fold under ½" (1.3 cm) of fabric on overlapping end. Lap it around the other end; finish stitching welting to duvet cover front. Follow steps 1 to 4 on page 39. Pin duvet cover front to back, right sides together; stitch, crowding cording. Turn right side out.

HOW TO MAKE A BUTTONED DUVET COVER

MATERIALS

- Decorator fabric or sheeting; fusible interfacing.
- Two zippers, each 22" (56 cm) long; buttons.

CUTTING DIRECTIONS

- Cut the front, back, and zipper strip as on page 39.

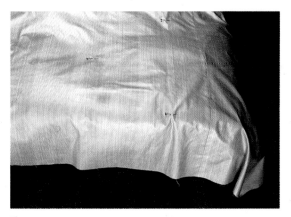  

1 Follow steps 1 to 4 on page 39. Place front of duvet cover on bed, with equal drop length at sides and foot of bed. Plan desired placement of buttonholes; mark.

2 Apply small piece of fusible interfacing under each of the buttonhole markings. Stitch buttonholes, and cut open.

3 Complete duvet cover as on page 39, step 5. Insert duvet; mark button placement on duvet under buttonholes. Sew on buttons.

HOW TO MAKE A TUCKED DUVET COVER

MATERIALS

- Decorator fabric, sheeting, or batiste.
- Two zippers, each 22" (56 cm) long.

CUTTING DIRECTIONS

Determine the finished size of the duvet cover (page 39). For the front and back of the duvet cover, cut one full width of fabric for a center panel and two equal, partial widths for the side panels; the panels are seamed together to make the front and back of the duvet cover. Two widths of fabric are needed for a twin-size or full-size duvet cover; three widths are needed for a queen-size or king-size cover.

The cut length of the front is 1" (2.5 cm) longer than the finished size. The cut width of the front, after the panels are pieced together, is 19" (48.5 cm) wider than the finished size, including 18" (46 cm) for the tucks and 1" (2.5 cm) for seam allowances. Cut the back of the duvet cover and the zipper strip as on page 39.

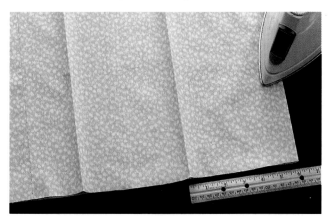 

1 Follow steps 1 to 4 on page 39. Wrong sides together, press foldline in center panel of pieced front, 2¾" (7 cm) from seamline. Press second foldline on center panel, 6" (15 cm) away from first foldline; press third foldline 6" (15 cm) away from second foldline. Repeat, pressing three foldlines on other side of center panel.

2 Stitch tucks 1½" (3.8 cm) from foldlines. For easier stitching, place tape on bed of sewing machine to use as a guide. Press tucks toward sides; outside tucks will cover seamlines. Complete as on page 39, step 5.

PILLOW SHAMS

For a coordinated bedroom set, sew pillow shams to match a duvet cover or bedspread. Pillow shams with ruffles, welting, or both can transform ordinary bed pillows into decorator pillows. They can also be used as decorative covers for accent pillows.

MATERIALS

- Decorator fabric.
- Two zippers for each sham; 12" (30.5 cm) zippers for standard-size shams, 14" (35.5 cm) zippers for queen-size, and 16" (40.5 cm) zippers for king-size.
- Cording, for shams with welting.

- Cord, such as pearl cotton, for shams with ruffles.
- Polyester upholstery batting, for shams with stuffed ruffles.
- Lightweight lining fabric and polyester fleece, for flanged shams.

Pillow shams with welting are a popular, classic style. Cut the sham fronts, backs, and zipper strips as for shams with ruffles on page 48. Cut the welting strips and construct the shams as for duvet covers on page 44.

Ruffled pillow shams (opposite) are romantic and feminine in style. For a new look, make shams with stuffed ruffles. For both styles, follow the instructions on page 48. If desired, welting may be used with ruffles; apply the welting first, then the ruffle.

Flanged pillow shams (page 49) are simple in styling and easy to sew. Flanges have been sponged (page 113).

HOW TO MAKE A SHAM WITH A RUFFLE

CUTTING DIRECTIONS

Determine the finished size of a pillow sham by measuring around the pillow for length and width, and dividing these measurements by two (page 27). The cut length and cut width of the sham front is 1" (2.5 cm) wider and longer than the finished size. Cut the sham back the same width as the front, and 1½" (3.8 cm) shorter than the front. Cut a zipper strip 3½" (9 cm) wide and the same length as the cut width of the back. Cut the fabric strips for the ruffle as for a duvet cover with a ruffle (page 42).

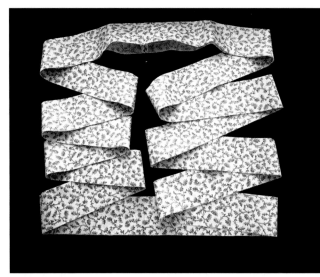

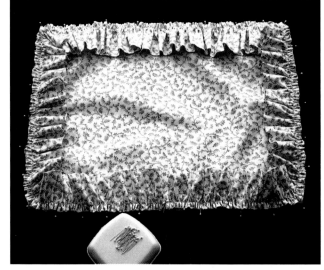

1 Stitch fabric strips for ruffle together in ¼" (6 mm) seams, right sides together. Stitch ends of ruffle strip together, forming a continuous strip. Fold pieced strip in half lengthwise, wrong sides together; press.

2 Finish as in steps 2 to 4 for duvet cover with ruffle (page 42), distributing gathers evenly on all four sides of sham.

HOW TO MAKE A SHAM WITH A STUFFED RUFFLE

CUTTING DIRECTIONS

Cut front, back, and zipper strip as for sham with ruffle, above. Cut fabric strips and polyester upholstery batting for stuffed ruffle as for duvet cover with stuffed ruffle (page 43).

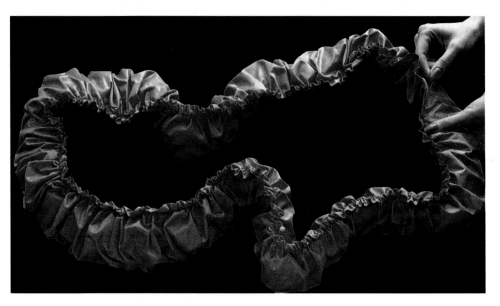

Stitch fabric strips for the ruffle together in ¼" (6 mm) seams, right sides together. Whipstitch ends of batting together and stitch ends of ruffle together, forming continuous strips. Fold ruffle strip in half lengthwise, wrong sides together, encasing batting. Finish as in steps 3 and 4 for duvet cover with stuffed ruffle (page 43).

CUTTING DIRECTIONS

For a flanged pillow sham, the center portion of the sham is equal to the measurements around the pillow, in length and width, divided by two (page 27). The cut length and cut width of the sham front is 7" (18 cm) wider and longer than the center portion. Cut one piece of polyester fleece and one of lining the same size as the sham front. Cut the sham back the same width as the front and 3" (7.5 cm) shorter than the front. Cut a zipper strip 5" (12.5 cm) wide and the same length as the cut width of the back. If welting is desired, cut fabric strips as on page 44.

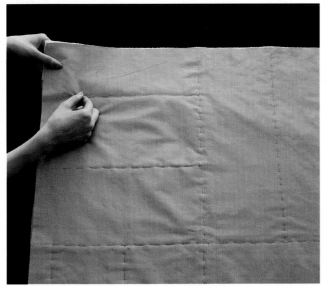

1 Follow steps 1 to 4 on page 39 for duvet covers. Baste sham front, fleece, and lining together in rows about 6" (15 cm) apart, starting at center and working toward edges.

2 Place sham front over sham back. Mark rounded corners, if desired, using a saucer; trim.

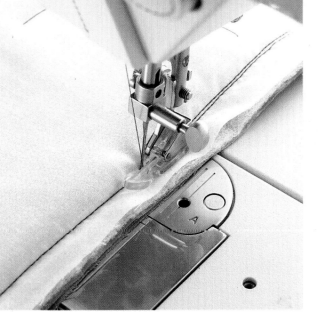

3 Make and apply welting to sham front as on page 44, if welting is desired. Stitch sham front to sham back, right sides together.

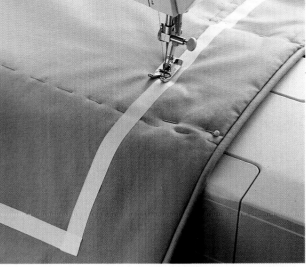

4 Turn sham right side out; steam edges. To mark flange, place artist's tape or transparent tape on sham front, with inner edge of tape 3" (7.5 cm) from welted seams. Pin layers together. Topstitch along edge of tape; remove tape. Insert pillow.

BED SKIRTS

For a coordinated ensemble, bed skirts are used with duvet covers and quilts. Designed to hide the box spring and legs of a bed, they can also be used to give the bed an attractive, finished look when a full-length bedspread is folded back. Choose from several styles, including gathered, tailored, and pleated. For best results, attach the bed skirt to a fitted sheet to prevent the skirt from shifting out of position. When bed skirts are used on beds with footboards, the skirt is split at the corners.

MATERIALS

- Decorator fabric.
- Fitted sheet.
- Cord, such as pearl cotton, for gathered bed skirt.

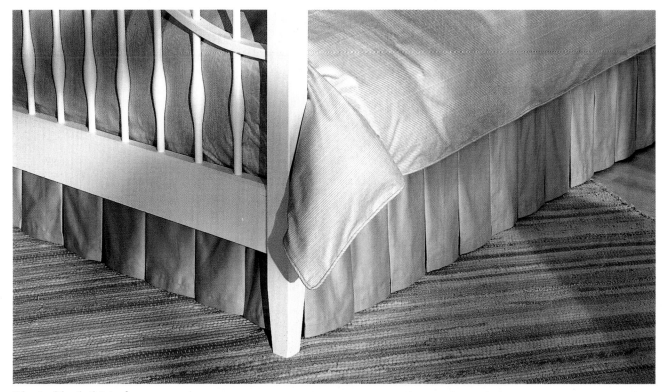

Pleated bed skirts have uniformly spaced pleats at the foot and sides. The pleats may be pressed for a crisp look or left unpressed for a softer look.

Tailored bed skirts feature pleats at the corners and at the center of each side.

Gathered bed skirts are evenly shirred for a more romantic look.

Gathered bed skirts add a look of softness to the bedroom. Classic in style, they are especially suitable for traditional decorating.

The bed skirt is attached to a fitted sheet to prevent the skirt from shifting out of position. For a bed with a footboard, a split-corner skirt can be sewn in three sections and attached to the fitted sheet. For this style, the sections are hemmed on both sides and butted together at the corners. If the bed does not have a footboard, the bed skirt is sewn in one continuous strip.

HOW TO MAKE A GATHERED BED SKIRT

CUTTING DIRECTIONS

For a bed without a footboard, the cut width of the bed skirt is two to three times the distance around the sides and foot of the bed. The fabric may be cut so the lengthwise grain runs horizontally on the project, to prevent piecing, or fabric widths may be pieced together as necessary.

The cut length of the bed skirt is equal to the distance from the top of the box spring to the floor plus 2" (5 cm) for hem and seam allowances and for ½" (1.3 cm)

clearance at the floor.

To make a split-corner gathered bed skirt for a bed with a footboard, the cut width for each of the two side sections is two-and-one-half to three times the length of the bed, and the cut width for the foot section is two-and-one-half to three times the width of the bed. The cut length of the sections is equal to the distance from the top of the box spring to the floor plus 2" (5 cm).

1 Place fitted sheet over box spring. Using water-soluble marking pen or chalk, mark sheet along upper edge of box spring on each side and at foot of bed.

2 Stitch bed skirt pieces together. For a bed without a footboard, stitch pieces in one continuous strip; for a bed with a footboard, stitch pieces in three sections. Finish seam allowances by zigzagging or serging. Press and stitch 1" (2.5 cm) double-fold hems at sides and lower edge.

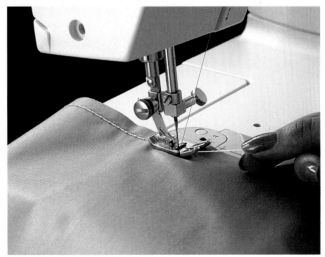

3 Zigzag over a cord at upper edge of skirt, within seam allowance, just beyond seamline. For more control when adjusting gathers, zigzag over second cord ¼" (6 mm) from first row.

Bed without footboard. Divide upper edge of skirt and marked line on fitted sheet into fourths; mark.

4 Bed with footboard. Mark corners at foot of bed. Divide upper edge of each skirt section in half; mark. Divide marked line on fitted sheet in half on each side and at foot of bed; mark.

5 Lay skirt right side down on top of box spring; match markings and pin upper edge of skirt to sheet, extending ½" (1.3 cm) seam allowance beyond marked line.

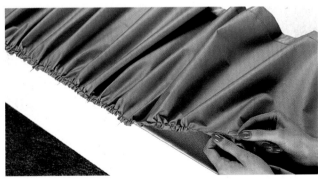

6 Pull on gathering cords, and gather skirt evenly to fit. Pin in place.

7 Remove bed skirt and fitted sheet from bed. Stitch bed skirt to fitted sheet, stitching ½" (1.3 cm) from raw edge; finish seam allowance.

Tailored bed skirts feature deep 6" (15 cm) box pleats at each bottom corner and at the center of each side and 3" (7.5 cm) pleats at the head of the bed. This bed skirt has simple design lines and can be used for all styles of decorating, from traditional to contemporary.

The fabric is cut so the lengthwise grain runs horizontally on the project. The design of the fabric is then turned sideways. If the fabric has a design that cannot be turned sideways, it is not suitable for this project.

Tailored bed skirts may be made for beds with or without footboards. For a bed with a footboard, follow the instructions for the split-corner bed skirt.

HOW TO MAKE A TAILORED BED SKIRT

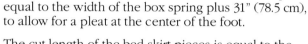

CUTTING DIRECTIONS

Cut three lengthwise pieces from one width of fabric, one piece for each side and one for the foot of the bed. Cut one piece for each side of the bed, with the cut width of each piece equal to the length of the box spring plus 23½" (59.8 cm). This allows for pleating, seam allowance, and hem allowance. For a twin-size, full-size, or queen-size bed, cut one piece for the foot of the bed, with the cut width of the piece equal to the width of the box spring plus 19" (48.5 cm). For a king-size bed, cut one piece, with the cut width of the piece equal to the width of the box spring plus 31" (78.5 cm), to allow for a pleat at the center of the foot.

The cut length of the bed skirt pieces is equal to the distance from the top of the box spring to the floor plus 2" (5 cm). This allows for the hem and seam allowances and for ½" (1.3 cm) clearance at the floor.

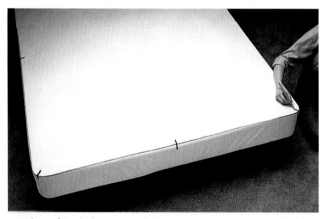

1 Place fitted sheet over box spring. Using water-soluble marking pen or chalk, mark sheet along upper edge of box spring on each side and at foot of bed. Mark corners at center of curve. Mark centers of side and foot sections.

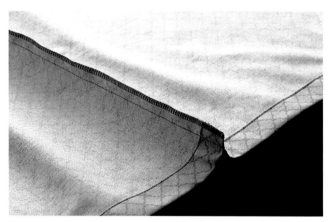

2 Press and stitch 1" (2.5 cm) double-fold hems at lower edge and sides at head of bed. Stitch bed skirt pieces together; finish seam allowances.

3 Position bed skirt so center of fabric is placed at center of foot. Fold pleats in place at markings as shown, with 3" (7.5 cm) on each side of pleat; pin to box spring with seam allowance extending above upper edge. Seams will be hidden in pleats.

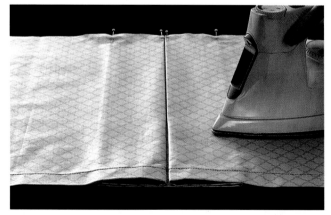

4 Remove bed skirt from box spring, repositioning pins to secure pleats. Press pleats in place, with even pleat depth from upper edge to lower edge. Machine-baste ½" (1.3 cm) from upper edge, securing pleats.

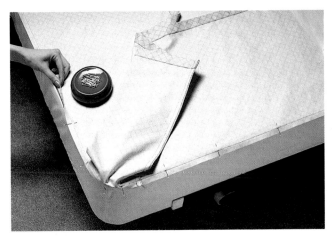

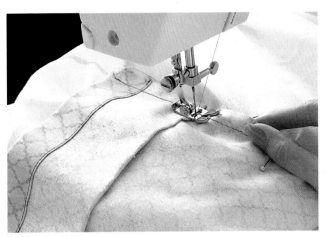

5 Lay skirt right side down on top of box spring. Pin upper edge of bed skirt to sheet, extending ½" (1.3 cm) seam allowance beyond marked line.

6 Remove bed skirt and fitted sheet from bed. Stitch bed skirt to sheet, stitching ½" (1.3 cm) from raw edge; finish seam allowance.

HOW TO MAKE A SPLIT-CORNER TAILORED BED SKIRT

CUTTING DIRECTIONS

Cut three lengthwise pieces from one width of fabric, one piece for each side and one for the foot of the bed. Cut one piece for each side of the bed, with the cut width of each piece equal to the length of the box spring plus 28" (71 cm). This allows for pleating and hem allowances. For a twin-size, full-size, or queen-size bed, cut one piece for the foot of the bed, with the cut width of the piece equal to the width of the box spring plus 16" (40.5 cm). For a king-size bed, cut one piece,

with the cut width of the piece equal to the width of the box spring plus 28" (71 cm), to allow for a pleat at the center of the foot.

The cut length of the bed skirt pieces is equal to the distance from the top of the box spring to the floor plus 2" (5 cm). This allows for the hem and seam allowances and for ½" (1.3 cm) clearance at the floor.

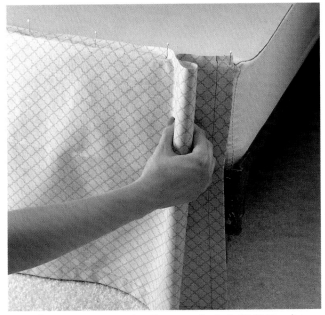

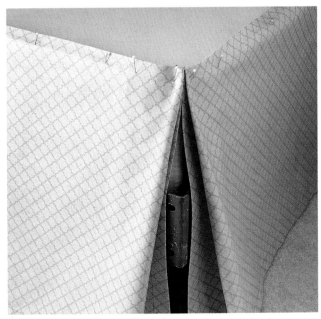

1 Follow step 1, opposite. Press and stitch 1" (2.5 cm) double-fold hems at lower edge and side seams. Position bed skirt piece for foot of bed so center of fabric is placed at center of foot. Fold pleats in place at markings as shown, with 3" (7.5 cm) on each side of pleat; pin to box spring with seam allowance extending above upper edge.

2 Pin side pieces to sheet, butting hemmed edges together and folding pleat at corner; pin. Fold and pin pleat at center of each side. Finish bed skirt as in steps 4 to 6, opposite.

A pleated bed skirt is a traditional style that works well for many room decors. The pleats may be pressed in place for a crisp, tailored look or left unpressed for a softer look. Pleated bed skirts may be made for beds with or without footboards. For a bed with a footboard, follow the instructions for the split-corner bed skirt.

HOW TO MAKE A PLEATED BED SKIRT

CUTTING DIRECTIONS

The amount of fullness in a pleated bed skirt is three times the distance around the sides and foot of the bed. For best results, plan the pleating so the foot of the bed will be divided evenly into pleats, with one pleat at each corner. A twin-size bed can be divided evenly into pleats spaced 6½" (16.3 cm) apart, with a 3¼" (8.25 cm) depth on each side of the box pleat. A full-size, queen-size, or king-size bed can be divided evenly into pleats spaced 6" (15 cm) apart, with a 3" (7.5 cm) depth on each side.

Cut the fabric so the lengthwise grain runs horizontally on the project whenever possible; the design of the fabric is then turned sideways. Cut three lengthwise pieces from one width of fabric, one piece for each side and one for the foot of the bed. For a twin-size, full-size, or queen-size bed, the cut width of each piece is three times the *length* of the mattress plus 10" (25.5 cm) for seam allowances, hem allowances, and ease. For a king-size bed, the cut width of each piece is three times the *width* of the mattress plus 12" (30.5 cm).

If the design of the fabric cannot be turned sideways, fabric widths may be pieced together as necessary. You will need to plan the placement of the seams so they can be concealed in the pleats as in step 3, below.

The cut length of the bed skirt is equal to the distance from the top of the box spring to the floor plus 2" (5 cm). This allows for the hem and seam allowances and for ½" (1.3 cm) clearance at the floor.

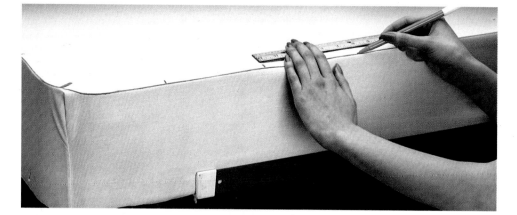

1 Place fitted sheet over box spring. Using water-soluble marking pen or chalk, mark sheet along upper edge of box spring at each side and at foot of bed. Mark corners at center of curve. Divide and mark line at foot of bed for evenly spaced pleats. Mark pleat spacing on sides equal to pleat spacing at foot.

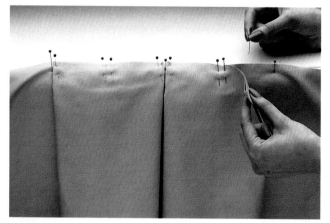

2 Press and stitch 1" (2.5 cm) double-fold hems at lower edges of bed skirt pieces. Position one bed skirt piece so center of fabric is placed at center of foot. Fold pleats in place from center of foot to corners, with depth on each side of pleat equal to one-half the distance between pleats; pin to box spring with seam allowance extending above upper edge.

3 Trim fabric 3½" (9 cm) beyond pleat foldline so seam will be concealed in pleat; for twin-size bed skirt, trim 3¾" (9.5 cm) beyond foldline. Pin side piece to foot piece, pinning along ½" (1.3 cm) seam allowance. Pin pleats in place on side of bed. Repeat for other side.

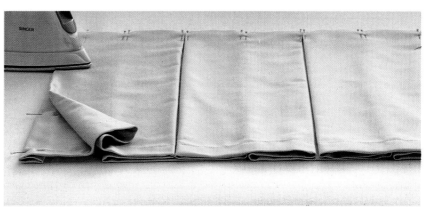

4 Trim fabric 2" (5 cm) beyond the desired endpoint at head of bed. Pin 1" (2.5 cm) double-fold side hems in place.

5 Remove bed skirt from box spring, repositioning pins to secure pleats. Press pleats in place, if desired, with even pleat depth from upper edge to lower edge.

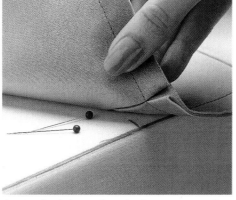

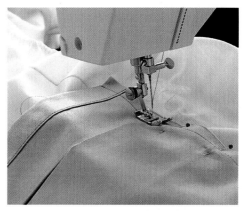

6 Stitch seams and side hems; finish the seam allowances. Machine-baste pleats in place ½" (1.3 cm) from upper edge.

7 Lay bed skirt right side down on top of box spring. Pin upper edge of bed skirt to fitted sheet, extending ½" (1.3 cm) seam allowance beyond marked line.

8 Remove bed skirt and fitted sheet from bed. Stitch bed skirt to sheet, stitching ½" (1.3 cm) from raw edge; finish seam allowance.

HOW TO MAKE A SPLIT-CORNER PLEATED BED SKIRT

CUTTING DIRECTIONS

Cut fabric as for pleated bed skirt, opposite.

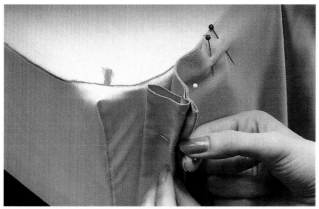

1 Follow steps 1 and 2, opposite. Trim fabric 2" (5 cm) beyond pleat foldline to allow for 1" (2.5 cm) double-fold side hem. Fold under 1" (2.5 cm) twice, and pin in place.

2 Pin side hem in place on next bed skirt piece. Butt hemmed edges together at corner; pin. Pin pleats in place on side of bed. Repeat for other side. Follow steps 4 to 8, above.

IDEAS FOR BED SKIRTS

Make a simple bed skirt uniquely appealing by adding a border of fabric or lace to the lower edge of the skirt. Or combine the basic styles, making a double-layer bed skirt that consists of two skirts. For a double-layer bed skirt, make the underskirt, following the bed skirt instructions for the desired style (pages 52 to 57). Then make and attach a shorter bed skirt, with the seamline of the second skirt ½" (1.3 cm) above the previous seamline.

Double-ruffle bed skirt *is made by using gathered bed skirts (page 52) in two lengths.*

Bordered bed skirt *is made by piecing a fabric border at the lower edge. When cutting the fabric, allow for the extra seam allowances.*

Lace-edged bed skirt is made by applying a flat lace trim to the lower edge of the bed skirt, following the instructions for bedspreads (page 33).

Flat-overlay bed skirt is made by using a tailored bed skirt (page 54) for the top layer and a gathered bed skirt (page 52) for the bottom layer. Interface the overlay for added body, and eliminate the pleats at the center of the sides, if desired.

BED SURROUNDS

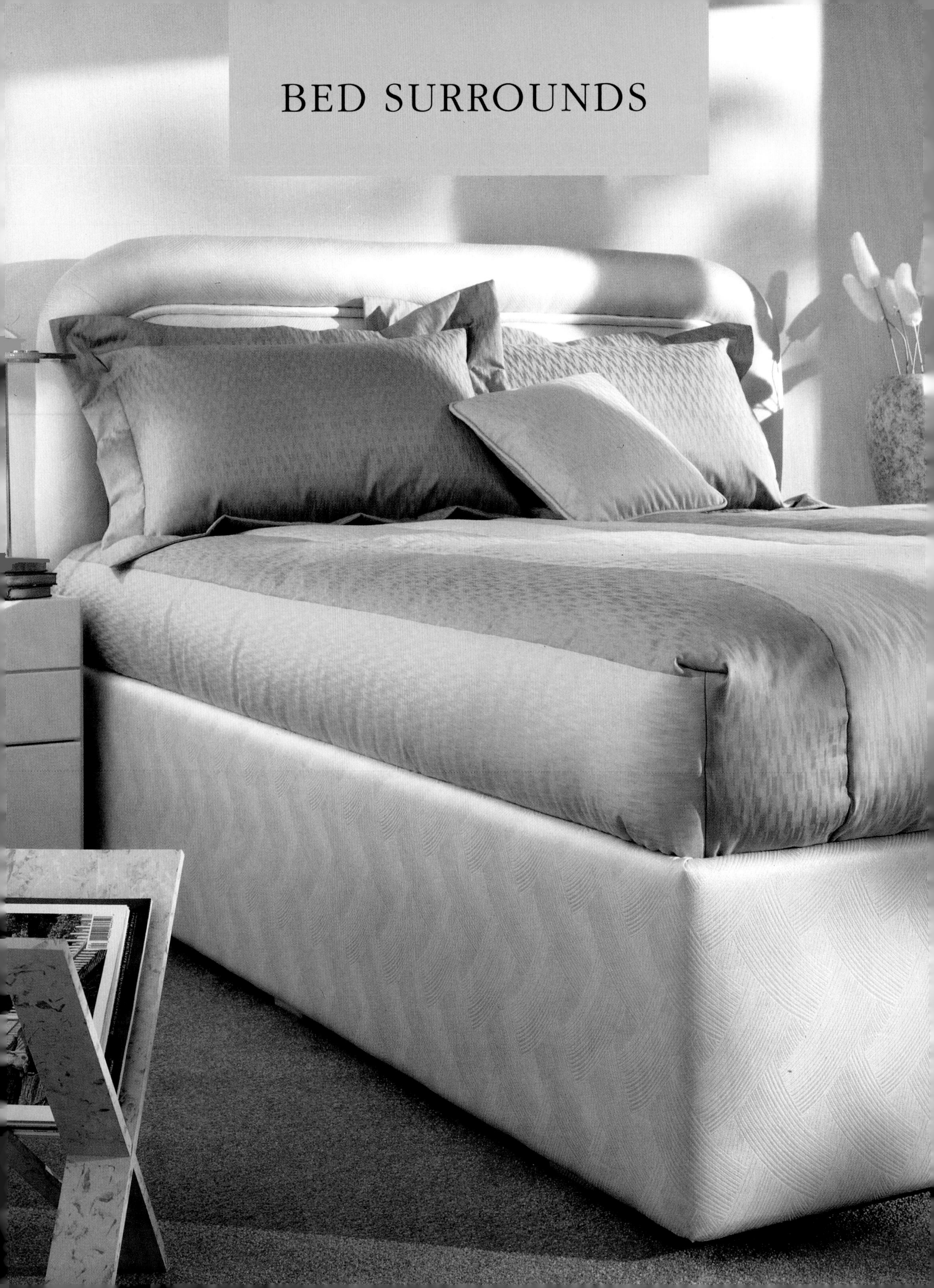

Bed surrounds are sleek and contemporary. The padded frame surrounds the box spring of the mattress for the look of a platform bed. Bed surrounds are often used with fitted bedspreads (page 34), but also look good with duvet covers (page 38) and comforter-length bedspreads (page 28).

HOW TO MAKE A BED SURROUND

MATERIALS

- Decorator fabric, length equal to distance around sides and foot of bed plus 8" (20.5 cm).

- ½" (1.3 cm) plywood for bed frame; two-foot length of 2 × 4 for legs.

- ½" (1.3 cm) polyurethane foam.

- Eight 2" (5 cm) angle irons, for corners at foot of bed and for attaching bed surround to headboard.

- Four angle irons, to attach bed surround to frame of bed (page 63, step 2); size will depend on bed frame.

- 6 × ½" (1.3 cm) screws; heavy-duty stapler and ½" (1.3 cm) staples (electric stapler is recommended).

- Twelve 1½" (3.8 cm) corner braces, for attaching legs.

- Drill, for predrilling screw holes; screwdriver; bolts.

CUTTING DIRECTIONS

Cut two boards for sides of bed, with each board equal to the length of mattress plus 1½" (3.8 cm). Cut one board for foot of bed, equal to width of mattress plus 2" (5 cm). These lengths allow for 1" (2.5 cm) clearance between the mattress and the bed surround. The width of the boards is equal to the distance from the top of the box spring to the floor. When supported on its legs, the top of the bed surround is higher than the box spring. Cut six legs from 2 × 4. Each leg should be approximately 3½" × 3½" (9 × 9 cm).

Cut fabric, with the length of the piece equal to distance around bed frame plus 8" (20.5 cm). The width of the piece is equal to two times the width of the boards plus 4" (10 cm).

Cut foam to same length as fabric. The width of foam is equal to width of plywood boards plus 5" (12.5 cm).

1 Draw line on one long side of each plywood board 2" (5 cm) from the edge. Matching lines, position footboard inside side boards. Secure boards, using angle irons and ½" (1.3 cm) screws; predrill holes for screws as in step 3 on page 106. Sand upper and lower corners to round them off slightly.

2 Mark center line on footboard. Apply polyurethane foam to outside of frame, stretching foam evenly over top and bottom and stapling along inner edges.

3 Mark center of fabric with clip marks at top and bottom edges. Place fabric, right side out, over outside of frame. Bring edge of fabric over frame to inside; staple raw edge at center of fabric to marked line at center of footboard.

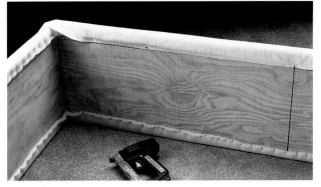

4 Working from center of footboard toward corners, staple raw edge of fabric along marked line at 10" (25.5 cm) intervals up to within 5" (12.5 cm) of each corner; keep fabric taut, but do not stretch.

(Continued)

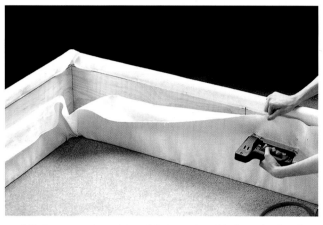

5 Lift frame up from floor, and position fabric under footboard. Smooth fabric around corner, stretching slightly. On side boards, staple raw edge along marked line at 10" (25.5 cm) intervals, starting 5" (12.5 cm) from corners and ending 5" (12.5 cm) from ends of frame.

6 Lift frame and position fabric under side boards. Staple-baste or tack fabric lightly in place on inside of footboard and side boards about halfway up the frame depth, keeping grainline straight.

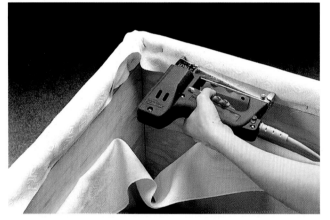

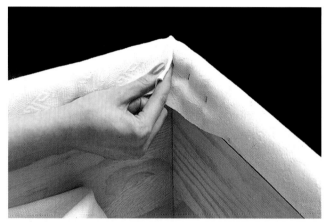

7 Apply staple at each corner of footboard. Staple along footboard at 1½" (3.8 cm) intervals.

8 Miter corners as shown; staple in place. Staple along side boards at 1½" (3.8 cm) intervals to within 5" (12.5 cm) of ends of frame.

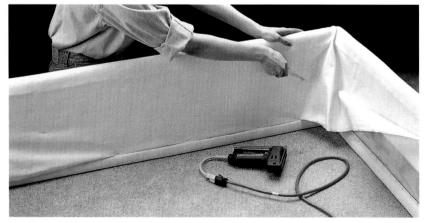

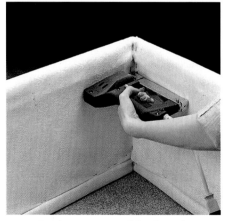

9 Turn plywood frame over so marked line is near lower edge. Fold remaining raw edge under; staple-baste or tack along folded edge at 10" (25.5 cm) intervals, stretching fabric taut and covering previous staples. Work from center of footboard to within 5" (12.5 cm) of corners, removing staples from middle of board as you come to them.

10 Staple corners and footboard as in step 7. Miter corners and staple along side boards as in step 8.

11 Bring fabric on outside of frame around end of frame; staple in place. Fold under fabric on inside of frame ½" (1.3 cm) from end of frame; staple.

12 Cover legs with fabric. Attach three legs to each side of bed surround, one at center of each side and one 10" (25.5 cm) in from each corner; legs should extend 1½" (3.8 cm) below lower edge of bed surround with cut ends of legs at sides.

HOW TO ATTACH A BED SURROUND TO A BED FRAME

1 Attach bed surround to headboard, using four 2" (5 cm) angle irons; predrill holes for screws. Center bed frame inside bed surround. Drill holes in legs of headboard to match screw holes in frame. Attach to frame, using bolts.

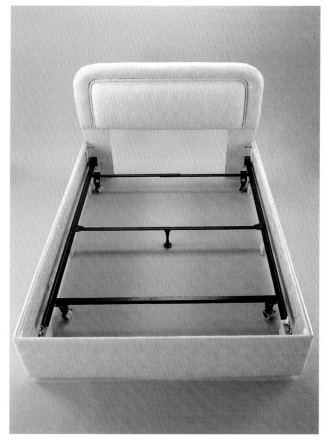

2 Attach bed surround to bed frame at holes in frame, using two angle irons on each side of bed; if necessary, drill holes in bed frame.

Finished bed surround is evenly positioned around bed frame at sides and foot of bed.

PADDED HEADBOARDS

For a custom look, make a fabric headboard to coordinate with the bedding, using basic upholstery techniques. Choose either a shirred or plain border to frame the edge of the headboard. Buttons can be added to either style for tufting, as shown on page 71.

MATERIALS

- Decorator fabric for the front of the headboard, and for the legs. Textured fabrics are easier to work with; for best results, avoid shiny or tightly woven fabrics.
- Lining for the back of the headboard.
- Polyester upholstery batting.
- Jumbo welting (page 44).
- ¾" (2 cm) plywood, cut to shape.
- 2" (5 cm) firm polyurethane foam.
- Heavy-duty stapler and ½" (1.3 cm) staples (electric stapler is recommended).
- Cardboard stripping, the length of the inner curve; foam adhesive; glue gun and glue sticks, or fabric glue; bolts.
- For shirred headboard, cord such as pearl cotton, for gathering.
- For tufted headboard, upholstery buttons; button twine; upholstery needle; drill and ½" (13 mm) drill bit.

CUTTING DIRECTIONS

The width of the headboard is equal to the width of the bed frame plus allowance for bedding. If a headboard is used with a bed surround (page 60), the width of the headboard is equal to the width of the mattress plus 3" (7.5 cm).

The height of the headboard is about 20" to 24" (51 to 61 cm) plus the length of the legs. The legs should be about 10" (25.5 cm) wide and equal in length to the distance from the floor to the top of the mattress. Make a paper pattern of the headboard. For a headboard with a plain border, the shape should be rectangular with rounded corners.

Determine the width of the border, and mark the inner curve on the pattern; a 4" to 6" (10 to 15 cm) border works well for most headboards. Mark a vertical center line on the pattern. Place the pattern on the wall behind the bed to check the size and shape; adjust as necessary.

Cut ¾" (2 cm) plywood, following the pattern; cut the headboard area and the legs from one piece of plywood. If you are making a headboard with a plain border, it is especially important that you cut accurately; smooth out the straight lines and shape the curves with sandpaper, if necessary.

Cut foam 3" (7.5 cm) wider and 1½" (3.8 cm) longer than the headboard area of the plywood; two pieces of foam may be joined together, using foam adhesive, if necessary. Mark the inner curve of the border on the foam. Mark a center line on the upper border of the foam.

Cut a rectangle of decorator fabric about 5" (12.5 cm) larger than the inner section. Clip-mark the center of the rectangle at the upper and lower edges. Cut a rectangle of polyester upholstery batting the size of the inner section.

For a headboard with a shirred border, cut a shirring strip three times the measurement of the outer curve and 6" (15 cm) wider than the width of the border. The strip may be pieced, if necessary.

For a headboard with a plain border, cut two side pieces and one upper border piece from fabric, with the cut width of the pieces equal to the width of the border plus 9" (23 cm). The length of the side pieces is equal to the height of the headboard plus the width of the fabric piece. Determine the length of the upper border as shown below.

For the legs, cut a fabric rectangle the length of the leg plus 3" (7.5 cm), and twice the width plus 4" (10 cm).

For jumbo welting, cut fabric strips and piece them together as necessary. The combined length of the strips is equal to the distance around the inner curve of the border plus about 5" (12.5 cm). Determine the width of the fabric strips as on page 44.

Cut the lining for the back of the headboard the same size as the headboard area of the pattern.

Upper border for plain headboard. Fold the paper pattern at each upper corner at a 45-degree angle to determine the placement of the seamlines on the border. To determine the length of the upper border piece, measure the distance between the marked seamlines at the inner corners (arrows), using a metal tape measure or a straightedge, then add twice the width of the fabric piece plus 1" (2.5 cm) to this measurement.

HOW TO MAKE A HEADBOARD WITH A SHIRRED BORDER

1 Plan button placement on paper pattern for tufted headboard. Mark plywood; drill ½" (1.3 cm) holes at marks.

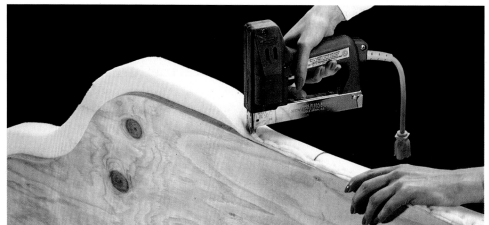

2 Affix foam to front of headboard, using foam adhesive, with lower edge of foam even with plywood edge and with side and upper edges extending 1½" (3.8 cm) beyond plywood. Pull excess foam over edge of plywood; staple to edge.

3 Staple cardboard stripping on marked line for border. If staples do not penetrate plywood easily, use hammer to tap them in place.

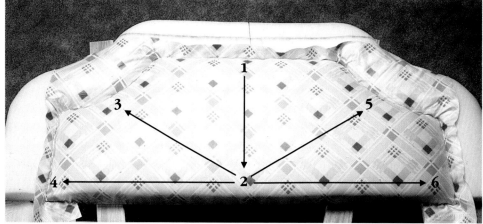

4 Place batting over inner section. Trim edges so batting does not cover cardboard stripping. Place decorator fabric, right side up, over inner section. Starting at center, pull fabric taut and staple to cardboard stripping in sequence shown; second staple is on back of headboard. Then staple at 2" (5 cm) intervals. Fold fabric at lower edge to back of headboard, clipping at corners; staple. Trim excess fabric.

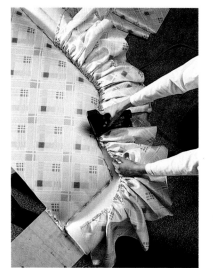

5 Gather one long edge of shirring strip by zigzagging over cord ½" (1.3 cm) from raw edge. Divide and mark curve and shirring strip into fourths. Working from right side, staple gathered edge of shirring strip to cardboard stripping, matching marks and adjusting gathers evenly.

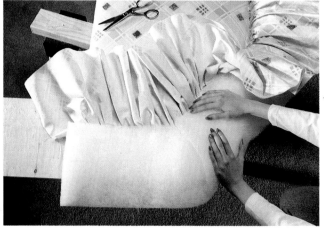

6 Pad border lightly with upholstery batting. Pull shirred strip and batting to the back.

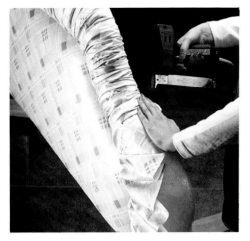  

7 Staple shirring strip to back, forming small tucks as you staple. Keep shirred area an even width on the front.

8 Make jumbo welting (page 44); trim seam allowances to ¼" (6 mm). Glue welting over stapled area to cover raw edges, stretching trim as you attach it. Secure with pins until glue dries.

9 Cover legs with fabric, folding under raw edges, except upper edge on back. Pull fabric tight, and staple in place; do not staple along upper edge on front.

10 Transfer button placement markings from paper pattern to fabric on headboard. Thread button onto 24" (61 cm) length of button twine. Fold twine in half; thread both ends into upholstery needle, leaving 5" (12.5 cm) tails. At markings, push needle from front to back through holes in plywood.

11 Pull twine until button has indented foam to desired depth. Pull twine to the side, stapling securely three or four times over twine so it will not slip.

12 Press edges of lining under ½" (1.3 cm). Finish back by stapling lining fabric over raw edges.

13 Drill holes in legs of headboard to match screw holes in bed frame. Attach to frame, using bolts.

HOW TO MAKE A HEADBOARD WITH A PLAIN BORDER

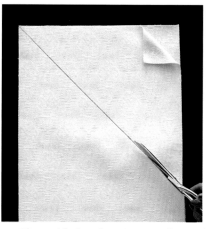

1 Follow steps 1 to 4 for headboard with shirred border. Measure in from ends of upper border piece, on lower edge, a distance equal to cut width of border piece; mark. Draw angled lines from markings to upper corners; cut on marked lines.

2 Place side border pieces right sides together. Cut upper ends of side pieces, through both layers, at same angle as upper border piece.

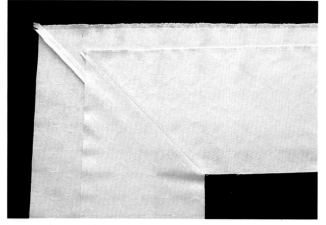

3 Stitch upper border pieces to side pieces along angled seamlines, right sides together, using ½" (1.3 cm) seam allowances. Press seams open.

4 Place layer of batting over foam in border area, wrapping batting around edge to back of headboard; cut inner edge of batting strips to fit inner curve. Butt pieces of batting together as necessary.

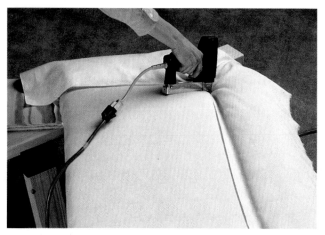

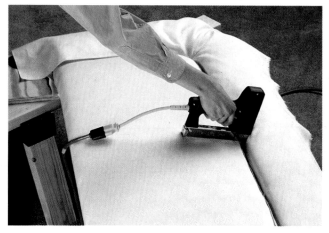

5 Place border fabric over foam, stapling corners in place through fabric, cardboard stripping, and foam; fabric should be stretched taut across top.

6 Apply a staple at center of upper border. Then staple at 1" (2.5 cm) intervals along inner edge of upper border, working from center to corners.

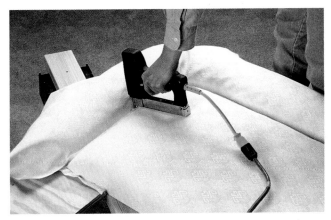

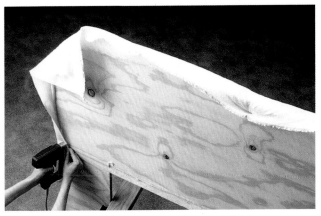

7 Align side border pieces over border area so grainline is straight. Pull fabric taut at lower corner of headboard area; staple in place, using one staple. Staple at 1" (2.5 cm) intervals from upper corners to lower edge of border. Clip excess fabric as necessary on curves.

8 Hold headboard in vertical position. Pull fabric taut to back of headboard at upper edge; staple at center, keeping grainline straight. Smooth upper border fabric on front of headboard toward corners; staple-baste at corner seamlines on back of headboard. Pull side border fabric taut to back of headboard at lower corner, smoothing fabric; staple-baste at lower corner on back of headboard.

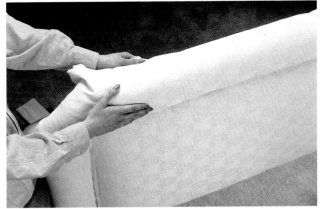

9 Smooth side border fabric toward lower edge, and pull to back of headboard; work from top to bottom, stapling to back at 4" (10 cm) intervals. Keep width of border even on front.

10 Smooth upper border fabric toward rounded area of corner, and pull to back of headboard; work from center to rounded area, stapling to back at 4" (10 cm) intervals. Keep width of border even on front.

11 Eliminate pull marks or diagonal wrinkles by removing staples as necessary; adjust fabric until border is smooth and even. Restaple.

12 Staple fabric on back at 1" (2.5 cm) intervals. At rounded corners, distribute ease as you pull fabric to the back; staple. On heavier fabrics, make tucks as necessary.

13 Trim excess fabric from front and back of headboard. Clip excess fabric at lower corners. Finish as in steps 8 to 13 on page 67 for headboard with shirred border.

BEDDING ENSEMBLES

With so many choices in bedding, the bed can be dressed in virtually unlimited ways. Select from the styles of bedspreads (page 28), duvet covers (page 38), bed skirts (page 50), bed surrounds (page 60), pillow shams (page 47), and padded headboards (page 64) to find the look you prefer.

Fitted bedspread *pairs up nicely with tailored and pleated bed skirt styles, such as this double-layer skirt. Flanged shams have been used for the bed pillows, and welted shams for the smaller decorator pillows.*

Welted duvet cover *with simple styling can be used with a bed surround instead of a bed skirt. To complete the ensemble, simple pillow shams, including welted and flanged styles, are used.*

Buttons *embellish both the duvet cover and headboard in this ensemble for a unified look. The gathered bed skirt and the ruffles on the duvet cover and shams coordinate well with the shirred border of the headboard.*

Window
Treatments

⚬⚬⚬

WINDOW TREATMENT BASICS

Window treatments provide privacy and light control in bedrooms, while underscoring the room's decorating style. Soft, flowing curtains, for example, can add to the lush appeal of a traditional room. And a rounded cornice can emphasize the lines of a contemporary room.

For rod-pocket curtains and rounded cornices, curtain rods are the only hardware needed. Install the curtain rods before making the window treatment. The rods can be mounted at the top of the window frame or on the wall. Whenever possible, screw the brackets into wall studs. Use molly bolts if it is necessary to install brackets between wall studs into drywall or plaster; the size of the molly bolt depends on the thickness of the wall.

Curtain rods, available in several widths, are used for simple rod-pocket curtains and valances (page 76). Select a clear or translucent curtain rod **(a)** for lace or sheer curtains, to prevent the rod from showing through and detracting from the fabric. The wide rods **(b),** known as Continental® and Dauphine®, can be used with rounded rods (below) for a different look.

Double curtain rods (c) consist of two rods with different projections mounted on the same bracket. When curtains and valances are used on a window, the inner rod is used for the curtain and the outer rod for the valance.

Pole sets, including contemporary metal **(d),** traditional brass **(e),** and wood sets **(f),** are available in several styles and finishes. Unfinished wood pole sets can be painted or stained, using any decorative technique (pages 111 to 121).

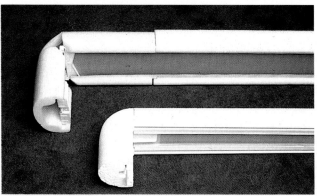

Rounded rods, known as Continental® Plus and Pinnacle®, are used in combination with wide curtain rods. These rods give a dimensional effect to rod-pocket curtains. Some rounded rods are also suitable for rounded cornices (page 85).

The heading (a) is the portion at the top of a rod-pocket curtain that forms a ruffle when the curtain is on the rod; the width of the heading is the distance from the top of the finished curtain to the top stitching line of the rod pocket.

The rod pocket (b) is the portion of the curtain where the curtain rod is inserted; stitching lines at the top and bottom of the rod pocket keep the rod in place. To determine the depth of the rod pocket, measure around the rod or pole; add ½" (1.3 cm) ease and divide by two.

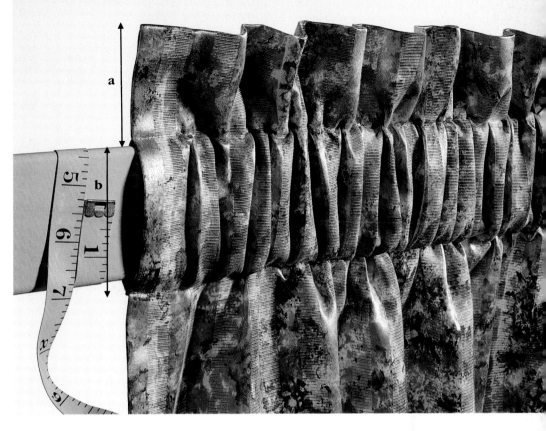

HOW TO INSTALL A ROD BRACKET BETWEEN STUDS

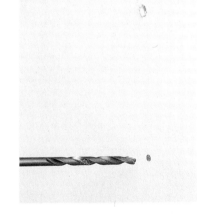

1 Hold curtain rod bracket at desired placement; mark screw locations. Drill holes into drywall or plaster; diameter of the drill bit depends on the size of the molly bolt. For heavy window treatments, use two molly bolts for each bracket.

2 Tap the molly bolt into the drilled hole, using a hammer.

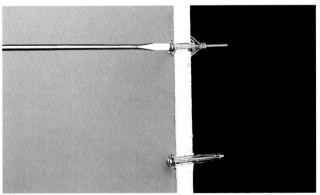

3 Tighten screw; molly bolt expands and flattens against back side of wallboard, preventing the molly bolt from pulling out.

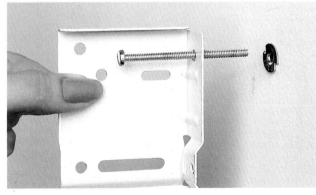

4 Remove screw from molly bolt; insert screw into curtain rod bracket. Align screw to installed molly bolt. Screw bracket securely in place.

ROD-POCKET CURTAINS

Rod-pocket curtains are a simple and versatile window treatment. From bishop sleeves to cafe curtains and valances, the look can be varied by the fabric choice, the choice of the curtain rod, the length of the treatment, and how the fabric is draped (pages 78 and 79). You may use a 1", 2½", or 4½" (2.5, 6.5, or 11.5 cm) curtain rod or a drapery pole set, depending on the look you prefer.

The basic construction steps of all rod-pocket styles are the same. Essentially, rod-pocket curtains are flat panels of fabric with stitched-in headings, rod pockets, and double-fold hems. For most windows, two curtain panels are used.

Before you sew, decide where you want the window treatment to be positioned, and install the curtain rod or pole. Measure from the bottom of the rod to where you want the lower edge of the curtain. To determine the finished length of the curtain, add the desired heading depth and the depth of the rod pocket to this measurement. This is what the curtain will measure from the top of the heading to the lower edge.

MAKING A ROD-POCKET CURTAIN

MATERIALS

• Decorator fabric.
• Curtain rod or pole set.

CUTTING DIRECTIONS

Determine the depth of the rod pocket and heading (page 75) and the width of the hem at the lower edge. A 4" (10 cm) double-fold hem is often preferred.

The cut length of each panel is equal to the desired finished length of the curtain plus the depth of the heading and the rod pocket, ½" (1.3 cm) for turn-under at the upper edge, and twice the width of the hem.

The cut width of the curtain is determined by the width of the window and the amount of fullness desired in the curtain. For sheer fabrics, allow two-and-one-half to three times the width of the window for fullness; for heavier fabrics, allow two to two-and-one-half times. After multiplying the width of the window times the desired fullness, add 4" (10 cm) for each panel to allow for 1" (2.5 cm) double-fold side hems. If it is necessary to piece fabric widths together to make each panel, also add 1" (2.5 cm) for each seam.

1 Seam fabric widths, if necessary, for each curtain panel. At lower edge, press under 4" (10 cm) twice to wrong side; stitch to make double-fold hem. Press under 1" (2.5 cm) twice on sides. Stitch to make double-fold side hems.

2 Press under ½" (1.3 cm) on upper edge. Then press under an amount equal to rod-pocket depth plus heading depth. Stitch close to first fold. Mark heading depth; stitch again at marked depth. As a guide for easier stitching, apply masking tape to sewing machine bed.

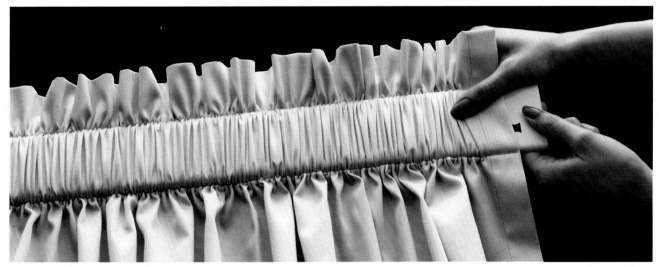

3 Insert curtain rod through rod pocket, gathering fabric evenly. Install rod on brackets.

VARIATIONS FOR ROD-POCKET CURTAINS

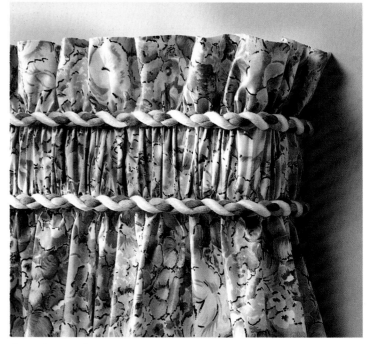

Curtains with trimmed rod pockets *have decorative cording or gimp along the rod pockets. Apply the trim to the installed curtain, using pressure-sensitive adhesive or double-stick carpet tape, trimmed to size.*

Tieback curtains *are rod-pocket panels (page 76), pulled back and held in place with tiebacks. For a new look, use craft ornaments, costume jewelry, silk flowers, or tassles as the tiebacks.*

Valances *are shorter versions of rod-pocket curtains (page 76) with 1½" (3.8 cm) double-fold hems at the lower edges. When using a valance over curtains, install it on a separate curtain rod. When using a valance between two side panels of curtains, install it on the same curtain rod.*

Tucked curtains *(page 81) feature tucks near the lower edge. For a coordinated look, use them with tucked duvet covers (page 41).*

Bishop-sleeve curtains *(page 80) are rod-pocket curtains that are elegantly pouffed. The fabric at the bottom of these extra-long curtain panels puddles lavishly onto the floor.*

HOW TO MAKE BISHOP-SLEEVE CURTAINS

MATERIALS

- Decorator fabric.
- Curtain rod; tenter hooks or cup hooks.
- Cording; bodkin or safety pin.
- Tissue paper, optional.

CUTTING DIRECTIONS

Cut two curtain panels, using one fabric width for each panel. Calculate the cut length of each panel as for rod-pocket curtains on page 77, allowing 2" (5 cm) for a 1" (2.5 cm) double-fold hem at the lower edge; add an extra 12" (30.5 cm) of length for each pouf and 12" (30.5 cm) to puddle on the floor.

1 Press under 1" (2.5 cm) twice on sides of panel; stitch. Repeat for hem at lower edge. Stitch rod pocket and heading as in step 2 on page 77.

2 Insert a cord into hem at lower edge, using bodkin or safety pin. Pull cord tightly to gather lower edge.

3 Insert curtain rod through rod pockets, gathering fabric evenly. Install rod on brackets. Determine location of poufs by tightly bunching panel with hands and lifting it to desired position.

4 Attach tenter hook or cup hook behind each pouf to hold tieback. Secure tieback tightly. Tuck tissue paper into pouf, if desired, to improve blousing.

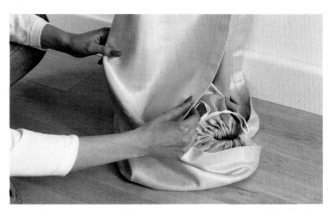

5 Arrange bottom of bishop-sleeve curtain, puddling fabric onto floor.

HOW TO MAKE TUCKED CURTAINS

MATERIALS

• Lightweight or sheer decorator fabric.

• Curtain rod.

CUTTING DIRECTIONS

Cut rod-pocket curtain panels as on page 77, allowing 16" (40.5 cm) for an 8" (20.5 cm) double-fold hem at the lower edge; add 9" (23 cm) of length for three tucks.

1 Seam fabric widths, if necessary, for each curtain panel. At lower edge, press under 8" (20.5 cm) twice to wrong side; stitch to make double-fold hem. With wrong sides of fabric together, press foldline for tuck 1⅝" (4 cm) from upper edge of hem.

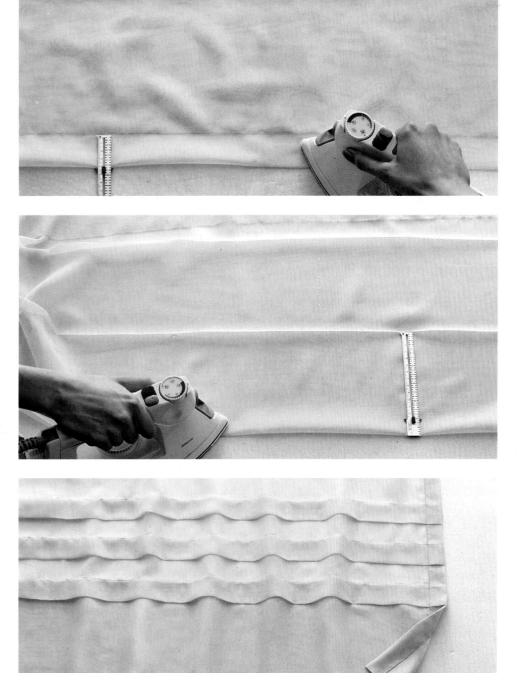

2 Press second foldline 6" (15 cm) away from first foldline; press third foldline 6" (15 cm) away from second foldline.

3 Stitch the tucks 1½" (3.8 cm) from foldlines. For easier stitching, place tape on bed of sewing machine to use as a guide. Press tucks toward lower edge. Press under 1" (2.5 cm) twice on sides. Stitch to make double-fold side hems. Complete curtain, following steps 2 and 3 on page 77.

Wide, rounded curtain rods, such as Continental® Plus and Pinnacle®, add dimension and depth to a rod-pocket curtain. To make a rod-pocket curtain for a rounded rod, make the front of the rod pocket deeper than the back, to allow for the "D" shape of the rod.

HOW TO MAKE ROUNDED-ROD CURTAINS

MATERIALS

- Decorator fabric.
- Rounded curtain rod.

CUTTING DIRECTIONS

To determine the finished length of the curtain, measure from the bottom of the rod to where you want the lower edge of the curtain; then add the desired heading depth and the depth of the *back* rod pocket.

The cut length of each curtain panel is equal to the finished length plus the depth of the heading, the depth of the *front* rod pocket, twice the width of the hem, and ½" (1.3 cm) for turn-under. Determine the cut width of the curtain as on page 77.

Determine the depth of the back rod pocket **(a)** by measuring the back, flat portion of the rod; add ½" (1.3 cm) ease to this measurement. Determine the depth of the front rod pocket **(b)** by measuring around the front, rounded portion of the rod; add ½" (1.3 cm) ease to this measurement.

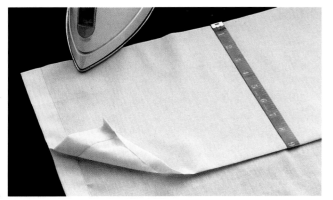

1 Follow step 1 on page 77 for rod-pocket curtains. Press under ½" (1.3 cm) at upper edge of curtain panel. From foldline, measure a distance equal to the *back* rod pocket plus the heading depth; press.

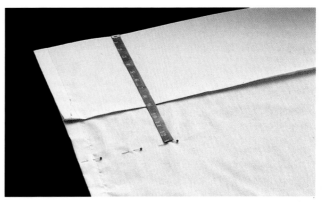

2 Measure a distance equal to heading depth plus *front* rod pocket from second foldline; pin-mark on wrong side of fabric.

3 Align first foldline to pin marks; pin fabric layers together. Stitch close to foldline.

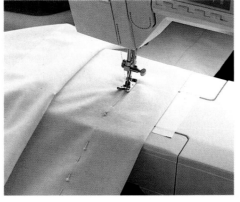

4 Refold panel at second foldline. Mark heading depth from foldline; stitch rod pocket. As a guide for stitching, apply masking tape to sewing machine bed.

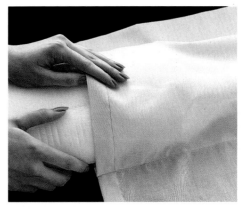

5 Insert curtain rod into rod pocket. Install rod on brackets.

ROUNDED-ROD CORNICES

Some rounded rods can be smoothly covered with fabric. These rounded rods work especially well with a contemporary decor, and may be used singly or in pairs as a cornice at the top of the window. The fabric is held in place with flexible tubing and straight pins. Follow the manufacturer's directions for installation.

HOW TO MAKE ROUNDED-ROD CORNICES

CUTTING DIRECTIONS

Measure around the sides and front of the installed rounded rod. Cut a 10½" (26.8 cm) strip of fabric, with the length of the strip equal to this measurement plus 1" (2.5 cm). Cut the strip on the lengthwise grain whenever possible to avoid seaming, or piece fabric widths together if necessary.

1 Center rounded section of rod on wrong side of fabric strip. Wrap fabric over the bottom channel, overlapping about ½" (1.3 cm). Starting at one end, place flexible tubing on fabric over channel; push into channel, using screwdriver.

2 Pull the fabric snugly around the front. Insert tubing into upper channel. Trim tubing even with ends of channels.

3 Snap covered rod onto wall brackets; attach molded returns, following manufacturer's directions. Fold fabric under ½" (1.3 cm) at ends. Wrap fabric around return; secure with straight pins, inserted from the back. Pleat excess fabric at corners; secure with pins.

Creative
Storage Ideas

COVERED BOXES

Boxes in all shapes and sizes can be covered with fabric to make pretty room accessories and provide useful storage space. Look for sturdy, smooth cardboard boxes with lids that do not fit too tightly. Computer-paper boxes and packing boxes work well. Chipboard or bristol board, purchased from stationery supply stores can also be used for making boxes. If the cardboard has a smooth, glossy surface on one side, this side can be used for the inside of the box, eliminating the need for lining.

For smoother edges on a corrugated cardboard box, wrap white tape around the edges of the box and cover any overlapped layers of cardboard or seams with white tape before applying the fabric. For durability, heavier cardboards should be used for larger boxes. Or boxes can be reinforced by gluing additional layers of cardboard to the sides before the box is covered.

Fabric may be applied to large surfaces with a spray adhesive, which covers the surfaces quickly without buildup. However, spray adhesive dries quickly, allowing little time for manipulating fabric. For this reason, fabric glue thinned with water works better for smaller areas. Apply the diluted glue to the fabric, using a flat paintbrush. When using spray adhesive, protect the surface from overspray by placing newsprint under the project.

Cover *an under-the-bed storage box to coordinate with your bedroom decor.*

CREATIVE STORAGE IDEAS

89

MAKING A BOX

MATERIALS FOR COVERED BOXES

- Chipboard, 10-ply poster board, or bristol board, for small boxes; 14-ply or 16-ply board, for larger boxes; or purchased cardboard or wooden bandboxes.
- Artist's knife.
- White tape, 1" (2.5 cm) wide.
- Mediumweight, firmly woven fabrics for outer fabric and lining; polyester fleece.
- Spray adhesive, intended for fabric use.
- Fabric glue, such as Sobo®, diluted slightly with water for easier spreading.
- Flat paintbrush or disposable foam brush for applying glue.
- Ribbon for covering raw edges of fabric on inside of boxes, optional.
- ½" (1.3 cm) fusible web, for bandboxes.

CUTTING DIRECTIONS

Determine desired finished width and length of box; add twice the desired box depth to these measurements. Draw rectangle to this size on cardboard; cut, using artist's knife or rotary cutter. Repeat for the box lid, making the lid ¼" (6 mm) wider and longer than box measurements; depth of lid may vary, as desired. When cutting with an artist's knife, it is better to use a few medium-pressure cuts rather than one heavy cut.

1 Mark the sides of the box on outside of cardboard, using a pencil. Score along the marked lines, using straightedge and artist's knife to cut cardboard lightly; do not cut through. Cut out corner areas of cardboard, using an artist's knife.

2 Fold sides, supporting cardboard on straightedge or edge of table along scored line, to keep folds straight.

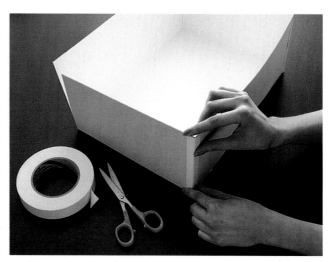

3 Tape sides together, using white tape. Construct lid, using the same method as for the box, except make lid ¼" (6 mm) wider and longer than box measurements.

LINING THE BOX

CUTTING DIRECTIONS

Cut the side lining piece wide enough to wrap around the four sides of the box plus 1" (2.5 cm) for overlap. The length of the side lining piece is equal to the desired depth plus ½" (1.3 cm) to allow the lining to extend onto the bottom of the box. Piece the side lining, if necessary, by overlapping and gluing pieces together.

Cut a piece of cardboard for the bottom of the box ¼" (6 mm) smaller than the length and width of the inside measurement of the box; round the corners. Cut the bottom lining piece 2" (5 cm) larger than the cardboard. Cut a piece of polyester fleece slightly larger than the cardboard bottom.

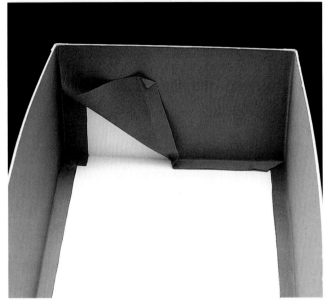

1 Apply spray adhesive to wrong side of side lining piece; affix lining to inside of box, overlapping ½" (1.3 cm) of lining onto bottom of box. Push fabric into corners and lower edge of box; miter bottom corners.

2 Apply spray adhesive to one side of fleece; affix fleece to one side of cardboard bottom. Trim edges even with cardboard.

3 Center cardboard, fleece side down, on wrong side of bottom lining piece. Trim corners of fabric diagonally. Wrap fabric around cardboard at corners and sides; glue in place.

4 Glue covered cardboard inside bottom of box.

COVERING THE BOX

CUTTING DIRECTIONS

For the outside of the box, cut two side pieces, with each piece equal to the width of the side plus 2" (5 cm); cut two end pieces, each equal to the width of the box end minus ¼" (6 mm). The length of the side and end pieces is equal to the depth of the box plus 1" (2.5 cm) to allow fabric to wrap around bottom of box plus the desired amount for wrapping around to the inside of the box. Cut fabric piece for bottom of box ¼" (6 mm) smaller than the width and length of the outside measurement of the box bottom. Cut a length of ribbon equal to distance around box plus 1" (2.5 cm).

1 Apply spray adhesive to wrong side of one side piece; affix to side of box, wrapping 1" (2.5 cm) of fabric around ends and bottom of box. Wrap the remaining fabric to inside of box; affix.

2 Turn box over. Miter corners on bottom of box; affix, using diluted fabric glue. Repeat for the remaining side piece.

3 Apply spray adhesive to wrong side of end piece; affix to ends of box, wrapping 1" (2.5 cm) of fabric around bottom of box and wrapping remaining fabric to inside of box at upper edge. Apply spray adhesive to wrong side of bottom fabric; affix to bottom of box.

4 Apply diluted fabric glue to one side of ribbon. Affix over raw edge of fabric on inside of box. Seal raw edges of fabric by applying diluted fabric glue.

COVERING THE LID

CUTTING DIRECTIONS

Cut a piece of fabric for the box lid, with the length of the fabric equal to the length of the lid plus four times the lid depth plus 1" (2.5 cm). The width of the fabric is equal to the width of the lid plus four times the lid depth plus 1" (2.5 cm). Cut a piece of fabric 1/4" (6 mm) smaller than the underside of the lid.

1 Apply spray adhesive to wrong side of fabric for lid. Center the lid top over fabric; affix. On ends, cut fabric 1/8" (3 mm) in from corner. On sides, cut fabric 1" (2.5 cm) beyond corner, angling to first cut.

2 Affix fabric to long sides of lid, wrapping it around the edge to the inside. Affix corners to ends of lid, using diluted fabric glue.

3 Affix fabric to ends of lid, wrapping it around edge to inside.

4 Apply spray adhesive to wrong side of fabric for underside of lid; affix. Seal raw edges by applying diluted fabric glue.

COVERING BANDBOXES

CUTTING DIRECTIONS

Trace the top of the lid on the wrong side of the outer fabric, polyester fleece, and lining. Cut outer fabric and fleece ½" (1.3 cm) outside the marked line; cut lining ⅛" (3 mm) inside the marked line. Trace the bottom of the box on the wrong side of the outer fabric; cut ⅛" (3 mm) inside the marked line.

Cut a strip of fabric for the lid, with the length of the strip equal to the circumference of the lid lip plus 1"

(2.5 cm); the width of the strip is equal to three times the depth of the lid lip plus ½" (1.3 cm). Cut ½" (1.3 cm) strip of fusible web the length of fabric strip.

Cut a piece of fabric for the box side, with the length of the piece equal to the circumference of the box plus 1" (2.5 cm). The width of the piece is equal to the height of the box plus 1½" (3.8 cm). Cut ½" (1.3 cm) strip of fusible web the width of fabric piece.

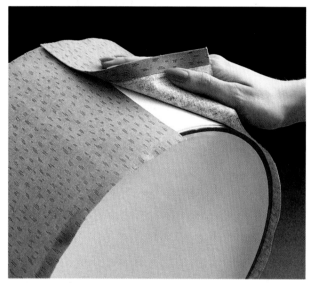

1 Turn under ½" (1.3 cm) along one short end of box side piece; fuse in place, using fusible web. Place side of box on wrong side of fabric, with ½" (1.3 cm) extending beyond bottom of box. Affix fabric to side of box, starting at short end and lapping folded end over raw edge; use spray adhesive for larger boxes, diluted glue for smaller boxes.

2 Clip lower edge of fabric at ½" to 1" (1.3 to 2.5 cm) intervals, to within ⅛" (3 mm) of bottom edge. Glue clipped edges to bottom of box. Apply spray adhesive to wrong side of fabric circle for bottom of box. Center fabric circle over box; affix.

3 Turn box right side up. Glue remaining fabric to inside of box. Glue ribbon over raw edge.

4 Apply spray adhesive to one side of fleece; affix to top of lid. Trim fleece even with edge of lid.

5 Spray other side of fleece. Center lid over outer-fabric circle for lid; affix. Clip fabric at ½" to 1" (1.3 to 2.5 cm) intervals, to within ⅛" (3 mm) of lid edge. Glue clipped edges to lid lip, using diluted fabric glue, lightly pulling fabric taut.

6 Press under one long edge of fabric strip for lid, wrong sides together, an amount equal to the depth of the lid lip. Insert strip of fusible web between fabric layers up to foldline; fuse in place.

7 Glue fabric strip to lid lip, placing fold at upper edge and overlapping ends of strip. Seal raw edge of fabric by applying diluted fabric glue.

8 Clip lower edge of fabric strip up to ⅜" (1 cm) from raw edge; clips should be spaced ½" to 1" (1.3 to 2.5 cm) apart. Wrap fabric around edge to inside; glue in place with clipped edges on underside of lid.

9 Apply spray adhesive to lining circle; affix inside lid, smoothing in place.

TRAYS WITH DIVIDERS

Fabric-covered trays are simply covered boxes (page 90) with dividers. They are convenient for use in dresser drawers, on vanity tables, and in the closet. Boxes divided into larger sections can be used to separate socks and lingerie items; those with smaller sections can be used for items such as jewelry. When used as liners in wire-grid closet storage units, they prevent small items from falling through the grid.

Determine the desired depth of the dividers. If you want the dividers to be flush with the top of the tray, subtract the thickness of the chipboard from the inside height of the tray.

Determine the placement for the sections. When making boxes with dividers, measure and complete each section before measuring for the next divider to ensure the correct amount of ease.

MAKING TRAYS WITH DIVIDERS

MATERIALS

• Materials as listed on page 90. Chipboard is recommended for this project.

CUTTING DIRECTIONS

Cut chipboard for tray following box instructions (page 90). For the outside of the tray, cut two side pieces from fabric, with each piece equal to the width of the side plus 2" (5 cm). Cut two end pieces, each equal to the width of the tray end minus ¼" (6 mm). The length of the side and end pieces is equal to twice the depth of the tray plus 2" (5 cm) to allow fabric to wrap around

bottom of tray on the outside and onto the floor of the tray on the inside. Cut a fabric piece for the bottom of the tray ¼" (6 mm) smaller than the width and length of the outside measurement.

Determine the placement of the sections. Sketch a diagram, including tray measurements, as shown in step 3. Cut chipboard for each divider, with the length of the chipboard equal to the length of the section plus twice the depth of each divider. The width of the chipboard is equal to the width of the section.

Cut a fabric piece for each divider 1" (2.5 cm) wider and longer than the chipboard.

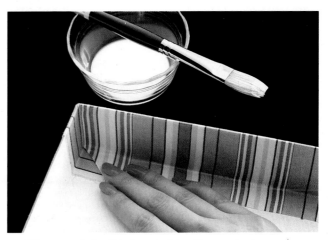

1 Make tray (page 90). Apply spray adhesive to wrong side of one side piece of fabric; affix to side of tray, wrapping 1" (2.5 cm) of fabric around ends and bottom of tray. Miter corners on bottom of tray; affix, using diluted fabric glue. Repeat for remaining side piece.

2 Wrap remaining fabric to inside of tray, mitering corners on floor of tray; affix, using diluted fabric glue. Apply end and bottom pieces as in step 3 on page 92. Seal raw edges of fabric by applying diluted fabric glue.

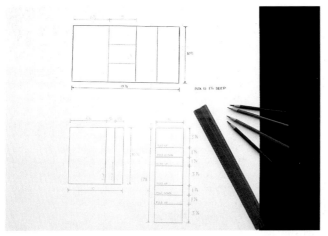

3 Sketch a diagram showing size of sections and placement of dividers; mark tray measurements on sketch. Cut chipboard for first divider, opposite. Mark foldlines on both sides of divider; label which direction divider will be folded on each line.

4 Score along marked lines, using artist's knife and straightedge to cut chipboard lightly. If divider will be folded up, score bottom of divider; if divider will be folded down, score top of divider.

5 Fold divider into shape. Apply spray adhesive or diluted fabric glue to wrong side of fabric; affix fabric to top of shaped divider. Wrap fabric around edges to underside of divider; glue fabric in place.

6 Glue first divider in tray. For next divider, measure section and repeat steps, checking fit of divider before covering it with fabric.

Increase your storage space by using storage chests in the bedroom. They are perfect for storing quilts, bed linens, or sweaters. You can make a wooden storage chest, or purchase one from an unfinished-furniture store. Divider trays at the top of the chest can be used for cherished keepsakes or other small items.

A wooden chest, built from plywood using basic tools, can be covered with fabric to coordinate with the bedroom decor. Casters and decorative handles, as well as support strips for a divider tray or shelf, as shown on page 102, can also be added.

The chest shown at left is made from ¾" (2 cm) plywood and is sturdy enough to double as a television stand or bench. The finished size of the chest is 34" wide × 21½" deep × 16" high (86.5 × 54.8 × 40.5 cm); the lid extends ½" (1.3 cm) beyond the front and sides of the chest. (The height of the casters is not included in this measurement.)

HOW TO BUILD A STORAGE CHEST

MATERIALS

- One ¾" (2 cm) 4 × 8 sheet of finish plywood.
- Piano, or continuous, hinge, 1¹⁄₁₆" × 30" (2.7 × 76 cm), with screws.
- 8 × 2" (5 cm) wallboard screws; fine sandpaper; wood glue; masking tape; rubber bumpers.
- Brass lid support (continuous-tension lid support is recommended); brass screws.
- Circular saw; drill; ¹⁄₁₆", ⅛", and ⁵⁄₃₂" (1.5, 3.18, and 3.81 mm) drill bits; phillips screwdriver.

CUTTING DIRECTIONS

From plywood, cut one front and one back, each 15" × 33" (38 × 84 cm). Cut two sides, each 15" × 19½" (38 × 49.8 cm). Cut one lid 21½" × 34" (54.8 × 86.5 cm). Cut one bottom, with measurement from front to back equal to 19½" (49.8 cm). The measurement of the bottom from side to side is equal to 33" (84 cm) minus twice the thickness of the plywood. Because the *actual* thickness of ¾" (2 cm) plywood may vary, the thickness must be measured in order to cut the bottom accurately. Some lumber yards will cut lumber to your specifications.

1 Sand wood surfaces smooth. Draw lines for screw locations ⅜" (1 cm) from lower edge of sides, front, and back pieces. Draw lines ⅜" (1 cm) from side edges of front and back pieces. Starting 1½" (3.8 cm) in from each corner, mark screw locations on marked lines at about 6" (15 cm) intervals.

2 Stand bottom piece on edge. Position one side piece so lower edges and sides are aligned to bottom piece. Using ⅛" (3.18 mm) drill bit, drill holes about 1¾" (4.5 cm) deep at marked screw locations.

3 Remove side piece; redrill holes in side piece, using a ⁵⁄₃₂" (3.81 mm) bit. Apply wood glue to joint area. Align pieces, and secure with 2" (5 cm) wallboard screws.

(Continued)

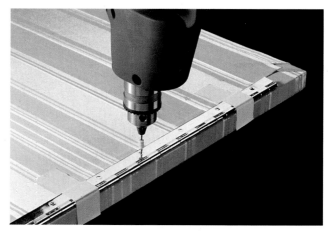

4 Repeat steps 2 and 3 for other side. Stand bottom and sides on end. Position front piece so side and bottom edges are aligned. Drill holes and secure with wood glue and screws as in steps 2 and 3; drill holes at lower corners first, then upper corners, then remaining holes. Repeat for back piece. Cover chest with fabric (opposite).

5 Center piano hinge on inside of lid, with hinge closed, so hinge edge is flush with plywood edge; tape in place. Predrill screw holes, using 1/16" (1.5 mm) drill bit, beginning at ends. To prevent drilling through plywood, mark length of screws on drill bit, using masking tape, and drill until tape reaches hinge.

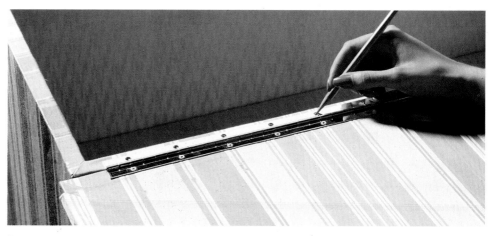

6 Open hinge and attach, using screws.

7 Center back edge of lid along back edge of chest, aligning edges and maintaining a small space between edges. Mark screw locations; remove lid. Predrill screw holes, using 1/16" (1.5 mm) drill bit, beginning at ends. Attach hinge, using screws.

8 Position lid support and mark screw locations, using pencil. Predrill screw holes and secure lid support, using brass screws.

9 Apply rubber bumpers to the underside of lid at front corners.

COVERING THE CHEST

MATERIALS

- Mediumweight decorator fabric; for best results, select a patterned or textured fabric.
- Primer for wood, if light-colored fabric is used.
- Spray adhesive intended for fabric use; fabric glue, such as Sobo®, diluted slightly with water; flat paintbrush for applying glue.

CUTTING DIRECTIONS

Cut a piece of fabric for the outside of the lid 4" (10 cm) larger than lid measurements; cut a lining piece 1½" (3.8 cm) smaller than lid. Cut lining and fabric for chest as for covered boxes (pages 91 and 92).

1 Apply primer to wood if light-colored fabric is used. Apply spray adhesive to wrong side of fabric for outside of lid. Center over top of lid, wrapping fabric around sides to bottom, forming miters at corners. Glue fabric in place at corners, using diluted fabric glue. Apply spray adhesive to wrong side of lining piece; affix to underside of lid. Seal raw edges of fabric with diluted glue.

2 Line and cover the chest as for covered boxes (page 91); miter and clip fabric at corners as necessary to wrap around to the inside of the chest.

ATTACHING SUPPORT STRIPS TO THE CHEST

MATERIALS

- Two wood strips cut from 1 × 1 pine stock; length of each strip is equal to measurement of inside chest width.
- 8 × 1¼" (3.2 cm) brass flat-head screws.

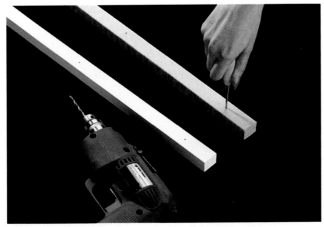

1 Drill four evenly spaced holes through each strip, starting 2" (5 cm) from ends, using 5/32" (3.81 mm) drill bit. Finish wood strips, or cover with fabric. If covered, poke holes through fabric at original holes, using awl.

2 Mark desired position of wood strips on front and back of chest. Screw strips to chest. Insert divider tray (page 96) or shelf.

CUSTOMIZING STORAGE CHESTS

Shelf or divider tray, *resting on support strips (page 101), provides more usable storage space.*

Decorative painting *(pages 111 to 119), such as sponging or spattering, makes a basic trunk unique.*

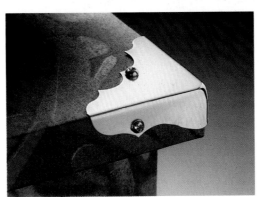

Decorative handles, *available in many styles, are functional as well as decorative.*

Brass corners *from woodworking supply stores add a decorative touch.*

Plate-type casters *can be attached to the bottom of the chest.*

Pickling *(page 120) coordinates a trunk to the bedroom color scheme, yet retains the beauty of the natural wood grain.*

SCREEN CLOSETS

Gain additional storage space for hanging clothes and accessories with this simple, four-panel screen closet. The screen, with shelving and closet rods on the back, is placed across a corner of the room to make an extra closet area. The end panels of the screen have casters and are hinged to swing open for easy access to the clothing. The screen may be stained or pickled (page 120), painted (pages 111 to 119), or covered with fabric (page 101) to fit the decor of the bedroom.

MATERIALS

- Two ¾" (2 cm) 4 × 8 sheets of plywood. For bests results, use finish plywood for fabric-covered screen, birch veneer for painted screen, or veneer in desired wood for stained or pickled screen.

- Two piano, or continuous, hinges, each 1½" × 72" (3.8 × 183 cm), with screws.

- Two wire shelving/closet-rod units, each 20" (51 cm) long.

- Four 3" (7.5 cm) angle irons; 8 × ⅝" (1.5 cm) flat-head wood screws.

- Two stem-type casters, 1½" (3.8 cm) high from bottom of wheel to base of stem.

- ¾" (2 cm) veneer tape, 57' (17.4 m) long, used to finish edges of plywood for painted, stained, or pickled screen; allow extra veneer tape if optional wooden shelves are added (page 109).

- Fine sandpaper.

- Primer, if plywood is to be painted or covered with light-colored fabric.

- Paint, wood stain, or 9 yd. (8.25 m) mediumweight fabric. For best results on fabric-covered screen, use textured or patterned fabric.

- Circular saw with a cutting guide; hammer; screwdrivers; tape measure; drill; ⅟₁₆" and ³⁄₃₂" (1.5 and 2.38 mm) drill bits; mallot.

- Shelf brackets, if wooden shelves are desired.

CUTTING DIRECTIONS

From plywood, cut two panels (A and D), each 22" × 72½" (56 × 184.3 cm). Cut one panel (B) 22" × 74" (56 × 188 cm) and one panel (C) 22¾" × 74" (58 × 188 cm). Some lumber yards will cut lumber to your specifications.

If wooden shelves are desired, as pictured on page 107, cut each triangular shelf with two 45-degree angles and one 90-degree angle. Short sides of shelf measure 22" (56 cm) long.

HOW TO BUILD A SCREEN CLOSET

1 Sand wood surfaces. If screen is to be stained or pickled, finish upper and side edges of panels with veneer tape, following manufacturer's directions. If screen is to be painted or covered with light-colored fabric, apply wood primer. Stain, pickle (page 120), or paint (pages 111 to 119) panels; or cover them with fabric as for chest lid (page 101).

2 Mark locations of casters on Panels A and D, centered on thickness of plywood and 2" (5 cm) in from outer edge of panel. Trim away fabric in caster area. Drill a hole the depth and diameter of caster stem into each panel, guiding drill bit at right angle to panel. Tap caster in place, using mallot.

(Continued)

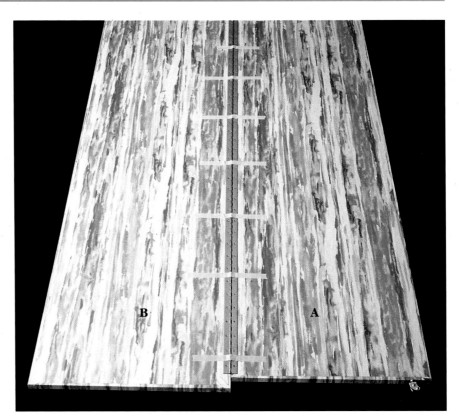

3 Position piano hinge on back of Panel A on side opposite caster; align hinge flush with upper edge, wrapping it around inner edge. Tape in place. Predrill screw holes, using a ¹⁄₁₆" (1.5 mm) drill bit. To prevent drilling through plywood, mark length of screws on drill bit, using masking tape, and drill until tape reaches hinge. Secure hinge with screws.

4 Open hinge flat. Butt Panel A up to Panel B, with panel fronts face down and upper edges even. Tape hinge in place. Predrill holes on Panel B, and secure hinge with screws.

5 Repeat steps 3 and 4 for Panels C and D. Fold each pair of panels at hinge, standing them upright, with Panel B butted up to front surface of Panel C at 90-degree angle. Attach Panel B to Panel C, using angle irons and wood screws; predrill screw holes, using ³⁄₃₂" (2.38 mm) drill bit.

6 Attach shelving units, following manufacturer's directions, to back sides of Panels B and C, 12" (30.5 cm) down from upper edge.

IDEAS FOR SCREEN CLOSETS

Conceal *hanging clothes behind the screen to gain closet space.*

Make *shelves for the front of the screen from leftover plywood, cutting them as on page 105. Apply veneer tape to the edges of the shelves, if desired. Stain or paint the shelves (pages 111 to 121) or cover them with fabric (page 101). Support the shelves on shelf brackets; use a level when you are mounting the brackets. Attach full-length mirrors to the end panels.*

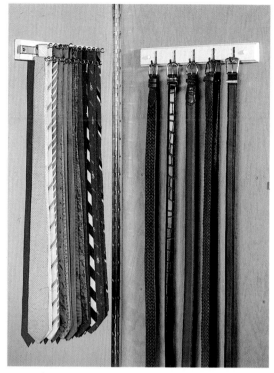

Store *belts, neckties, jewelry, and other accessories on the back sides of the end panels, using various types of hooks and tie racks.*

Finishing
Touches

FAUX FINISHES

Decorative painting is an inexpensive way to customize and embellish the bedroom. For a unified look, the walls, bedcoverings, and draperies can be painted to coordinate. Or vases, picture frames, lamp bases, and small pieces of furniture can be painted decoratively. Several methods for decorative painting are available. Choose the one that appeals to you or combine more than one technique for a unique look.

For sponging, use natural sea sponges to dab paint onto a surface; this creates a mottled, irregular appearance. Synthetic sponges should not be used, because they tend to leave identical impressions with hard, defined edges.

Another method for decorative painting is "ragging-on." This technique uses crumpled rags to apply diluted paint to the surface. Or use crumpled net, burlap, cheesecloth, or newsprint.

Spattering is applying a mist of color over a base coat of paint. When the color is spattered in a fine texture, the process is often called specking. Spattering and specking are easier when you are applying paint to horizontal surfaces rather than vertical surfaces, such as walls. You can spatter the paint on an entire project or mask off design areas before spattering.

Marbling creates the look of a marble surface with diagonal drifts of sponging or ragging-on. Veining gives the surface a more authentic appearance, simulating the fragmented cracks that occur in marble. To add the veins, paint is applied with the tip of a feather or fine fan brush.

Whichever technique you use, prepare the surface before you start painting. A finished wood surface should be sanded lightly, removing any shine, to ensure paint adhesion. An undercoat of primer should be applied to unfinished wood surfaces, unfinished wallboard, or ceramics (page 112).

For fabric painting, select mediumweight to heavyweight fabrics with at least 50 percent cotton, such as sheeting, poplin, and muslin, for good dye penetration. Avoid fabrics with polished or protective finishes. Prewash the fabric to remove any sizing.

When painting walls, protect the ceiling by using a painter's edge and cover the baseboards with newsprint and masking tape. Apply paint, working in 2-ft. (61-cm) strips from the ceiling to the baseboard. The paint can lap onto the covered baseboard.

Before using the decorative painting on walls, test the paint colors on a large piece of cardboard, such as poster board. Practice fabric painting, using remnants of the actual fabric you plan to use. By practicing first on scraps of fabric or cardboard, you will develop confidence and become familiar with the materials and techniques. Try different effects as you practice, by varying the amount of pressure you apply and the spacing between colors, until you develop a pattern that pleases you.

IDEAS FOR FAUX FINISHES

SELECTING PAINT

If you are painting on ceramics or unfinished wood surfaces or wallboard, you will need to use a primer as the first coat. For ceramics with glossy finishes, select a primer suitable for high-gloss surfaces.

Low-luster latex enamel interior paints are usually chosen for decorative painting on walls, furniture, and accessories. To create a less reflective surface, a matte latex paint may be used for the base coat. For furniture, a satin or semigloss enamel is recommended for durability. For small projects, acrylic paints, available in small bottles, may be used. A varnish may be applied for added sheen and protection.

For painting on fabrics, textile paints are used; depending on the consistency of the paint you choose, you may want to thin the paint with water for a more transparent effect. After painting fabrics, the textile paints are heat-set according to the manufacturer's directions.

The number of colors used and the contrast between colors will affect the look. Choose light colors for a watercolor effect, and choose colors of different intensities to give the surface a more dimensional effect.

The sequence in which you apply the paints will also affect the look. Frequently, the next-to-the-darkest color is used for the base coat, and the remaining colors are applied, working from the darkest color to the lightest. You may want to plan the sequence so the base coat and the top coat are shades of the same color; this causes the paints to blend for an overall mottled effect.

Magazine rack *is painted by applying two colors of paint, using the ragging-on method (page 115). A final coat of spray varnish adds luster and provides a durable finish.*

MATERIALS

FOR ALL TYPES OF PAINTING

- Primer, for painting ceramics, unfinished wood or wallboard.
- Paint for base coat in desired background color, amount according to square footage; base coat is not needed for painting on fabrics.
- Accent paints; 1 quart (0.9 liter) per color is sufficient to paint walls in a room.
- Paint tray for large projects or disposable plastic plate for small projects.

FOR SPONGING

- Natural sea sponge; use 2" (5 cm) pieces of sponge for small projects.
- Newsprint, for blotting excess paint.

FOR RAGGING-ON

- Rags, newsprint, net, cheesecloth, or burlap for applying paint to surface.

- Disposable foam brush.
- Latex paint conditioner.
- Small bucket for mixing glaze.

FOR SPATTERING & SPECKING

- 1" or 1½" (2.5 or 3.8 cm) synthetic-bristle paintbrush.
- Paint-stirring stick.
- Stiff brush with short bristles, such as toothbrush or nail brush.
- Table knife or palette knife.

FOR MARBLING & VEINING

- Metallic paint for veining, if desired.
- Turkey quill or fine fan brush.
- 3" (7.5 cm) synthetic-bristle paintbrush.
- Rag for blotting paint.

Walls *(above) have been painted, using the techniques of sponging and ragging-on (pages 114 and 115).*

Flanged pillow shams *(page 49) have been sponged (page 114), using textile paints. Apply masking tape inside the border while sponging to define the edges of the flange.*

Lamp and picture frame *are painted, using coordinating faux finishes. The lamp is sponged (page 114), and the picture frame, specked (page 115).*

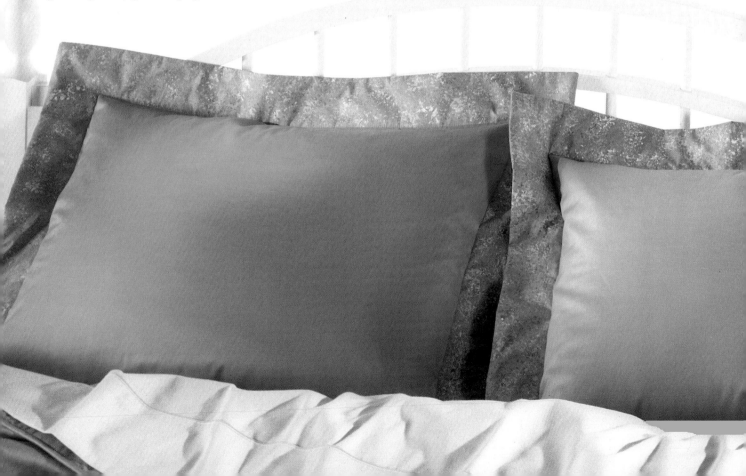

SPONGING

1 Apply base coat of desired background color to clean, prepared surface; allow to dry. Rinse sponge in water to soften it; squeeze dry. Pour small amount of first paint color into paint tray; tilt toward top of tray. Dab sponge into paint, taking care not to overload it. Blot sponge on newsprint until you get a light impression.

2 Press sponge gently onto surface, using quick, light touch; do not drag sponge across surface. Change position of sponge often for irregular impressions. Apply more paint to sponge, as necessary, blotting on newsprint.

3 Continue to apply first color to entire project until individual sponge marks cannot be seen. Stand back frequently to examine the work; fill in areas as necessary. If using more than one color, apply first color sparingly.

4 Allow first color of paint to dry. Rinse sponge and paint tray. Repeat steps for each color of paint desired. Apply the last color, filling in between previous sponge marks to blend colors.

RAGGING-ON

1 Apply base coat to clean, prepared surface; allow to dry. Mix glaze by combining one part paint with two parts latex paint conditioner. For translucent look, also add one part water.

2 Crumple rag or desired applicator, making as many ridges as possible. Apply glaze to crumpled material, using disposable foam brush. Use applicator as for sponging, opposite. Replace applicator as it becomes saturated.

SPATTERING

Protect work surface with drop cloths. Mix paints in small cups, combining two parts paint with one part water. Dip tip of brush into paint; remove excess paint on edge of cup. Hold stick and brush over project; strike brush handle against stick to spatter paint. Work from top to bottom in wide strips. Allow first color of paint to dry. Repeat steps for each color, as desired.

SPECKING

Dip ends of stiff-bristled brush into thinned paint. Tap brush onto piece of paper to remove excess paint. Hold brush over surface to be painted; flick bristles toward you, using knife or finger, spraying paint away from you. The closer to the surface the brush is held, the finer the spattering and the more control you have.

MARBLING

 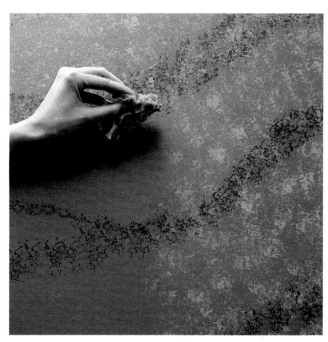

1 Apply paint in diagonal drifts, using sponging (page 114) or ragging-on (page 115). Soften drifts by gently blotting any wet paint with a tissue and lightly whisking a dry paintbrush over the surface.

2 Apply second color of paint or glaze in a lighter tone, blending textures and colors. If desired, embellish the marbeled surface with veining (below).

VEINING

 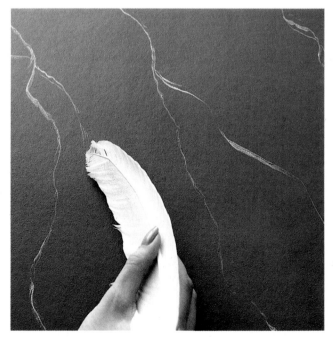

1 Thin paints with water, if desired, for a translucent appearance. Dip tip of feather or brush into paint. Remove excess paint on edge of container.

2 Draw tip of feather or brush lightly along surface, at 45-degree angle; use trembling motion, causing veins to waver or break off and reappear. Fork veins, and cross one over another. When crossing over a vein, lift feather or brush, and shift direction. To vary width of vein, twist wrist as you paint.

Sponging, ragging-on, and veining were used to achieve a marbled look. Paint was applied in drifts of color, using newspaper.

Sponging and veining were combined, using high-contrast colors for a bold impact and silver metallic paint for highlights.

Ragging-on was used to apply lighter colors over a dark background. Paint was applied in an all-over pattern, using a rag.

Spattering and specking were combined for a granitelike texture.

Sponging was used to create a mottled, even texture. Light colors give a watercolor effect.

DECORATIVE PAINTING

Express your creativity by decoratively painting some of your bedroom furnishings. The finished project, like the headboard pictured on page 23, can be a unique focal point of the bedroom, even if you start with garage-sale furniture or an inexpensive unfinished piece.

If the surface you are decorating is unfinished, apply a primer before you paint it. If the surface has been previously painted, sand it first, removing any gloss, to ensure good paint adhesion. For a smooth base finish, apply two or three thin base coats, sanding lightly between coats with wet sandpaper. After the decorative painting is completed, a coat of varnish or polyurethane sealer can be applied for a smooth, slick surface and added durability.

TIPS FOR DECORATIVE PAINTING

MATERIALS

- Primer, if surface is unfinished.
- Fine, wet-dry sandpaper.
- Enamel or acrylic paint in desired colors.
- Paintbrush for applying base coat; artist's brushes.
- Masking tape.
- Varnish or polyurethane sealer, optional.

Mark design, using pencil. Decorator fabrics and pictorial design books can offer design ideas.

Apply masking tape to define edges and sharp outlines; press tape firmly in place. Apply as little paint as possible, to prevent paint from bleeding under tape.

Apply paint to small areas using artist's brushes, such as ½" (1.3 cm) flat brush or small, round brush.

Create textured design, drawing cardboard strips, comb, or other household item through generously applied wet paint.

Experiment with your own creative methods. Finger-paint, using lots of paint on surface.

PICKLING

Add interest to unfinished bedroom furniture and accessories by applying colored stains, often called pickling. Because these stains are transparent, you can color-coordinate wood furniture to curtains and bedding, as in the chair and end table (opposite), without covering up the beauty of the wood grain. Pickling may also be used for wicker and sisal, as shown in the mirror frame and floor mat. Use a premixed stain or have stain custom-mixed at a paint supply store. Test the stain on the back or bottom of the item. If the color is too intense, you may add a small amount of mineral spirits to thin the stain. If the color is too light, the staining process may be repeated.

MATERIALS

- Unfinished wood, wicker, or sisal item; sand wood smooth, using fine sandpaper.
- Oil-based colored stain; mineral spirits.

- Soft cotton cloth; fine steel wool; tack cloth; paintbrush.
- Tung oil, varnish, or polyurethane sealer for wood; spray varnish or lacquer for wicker or sisal.

PICKLING WOOD

1 Prepare wood surface as recommended on can of stain. Apply stain with cloth, rubbing it into wood; allow to dry.

2 Rub wood surface lightly in direction of grain, using steel wool. Wipe surface thoroughly with tack cloth.

3 Finish wood as desired, using tung oil, varnish, or polyurethane sealer.

PICKLING WICKER OR SISAL

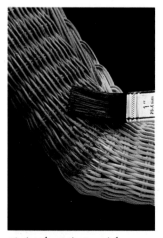

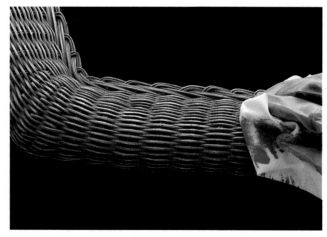

1 Apply stain to wicker or sisal with brush, working stain into crevices.

2 Remove stain from outer edges of wicker or sisal with soft cotton cloth, if desired, giving the item an antiqued look.

3 Finish, using spray varnish or lacquer, to prevent stain from rubbing off.

PORCELAIN FLOWERS & BOWS

Silk or polyester flowers can be crafted to resemble porcelain flowers. Porcelain bows, made using the same technique, can be added to the arrangements.

The flowers are painted with a base coat of matte-finish white aerosol paint, which provides a good background for all colors and adds body to the flowers; it is not necessary to apply this base coat to the ribbon if white ribbon is used. To porcelainize the flowers and bows, they are dipped in a setting agent and painted with acrylic paints. For the look of fine porcelain, thin the paint with extender. When extender is added, the paint spreads more smoothly.

Porcelain flowers and bows can decorate baskets or grapevine wreaths, or be used as an arrangement in a vase. Porcelain roses have a Victorian look, but other types of flowers may be used for other decorating styles, including contemporary.

MATERIALS

- Silk or polyester flowers; use flowers without plastic parts, or cover any plastic with florist's tape to ensure that paint will bond.
- Basket, grapevine wreath, or other object to be decorated.
- White ribbon for bows.
- Matte-finish white aerosol paint.
- Porcelain-setting agent.
- Acrylic paints in desired colors.

- Extender to thin the paint, optional.
- Clear aerosol glaze for porcelainizing; read cautions on label before use.
- Artist's brushes, #10 shader for ribbon; #8 flat or shader and #2 filbert or shader for flowers and leaves; #2 round for painting small details.
- Wire cutters for cutting flower stems; disposable plastic bowl for setting agent; disposable plate for paint palette.

Porcelain flowers and bows
*embellish picture frames, lamps,
wreaths, or other room
accessories.*

HOW TO MAKE PORCELAIN FLOWERS

1 Plan design of project, including bow. Pull blossoms and leaves from stem, or cut them, using wire cutter. Trim rough edges with small scissors. Spray each item with aerosol paint; allow to dry.

2 Pour setting agent into plastic bowl to depth necessary to dip flowers. Beginning with largest blossom, dip into setting agent. Strip off as much setting agent as possible by pulling petals gently between your forefinger and thumb.

3 Arrange petals as desired. Remove any excess setting agent with flat artist's brush to achieve a smooth coating. Clamp or hang blossom until dry.

4 Repeat for remaining flowers, then leaves. Allow items to dry overnight.

5 Thin acrylic paints with extender, if desired. Paint flowers, leaves, and porcelainized bow (opposite), shading if desired; allow to dry. Apply second coat of paint if brush strokes are noticeable; allow to dry.

6 Affix items to project, using setting agent and brush. Also apply setting agent to flowers, blossoms, and bow where items touch. Trim ends of ribbon.

7 Spray entire project with one or two coats of clear aerosol glaze.

HOW TO MAKE A PORCELAIN BOW

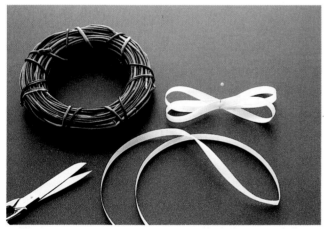

1 Loop ribbon in a figure eight, to determine desired size and number of loops; cut a piece of ribbon to this length. For knot and streamers, cut a second piece of ribbon to desired length.

2 Dip ribbons into setting agent, and pull through fingers to strip off as much as possible. Loop first ribbon in figure eight; place on table over second ribbon. Bring ends of second ribbon up over loops; tie.

3 Arrange bow in desired position, draping and twisting loops and streamers. Support ribbon with props as necessary. Allow to dry overnight. Complete project as in steps 5 to 7 (opposite).

INDEX

CREDITS

CY DECOSSE INCORPORATED
Chairman: Cy DeCosse
President: James B. Maus
Executive Vice President:
  William B. Jones

BEDROOM DECORATING
Created by: The Editors of
Cy DeCosse Incorporated.

Also available from the publisher:
*Creative Window Treatments,
Decorating for Christmas*

Executive Editor: Zoe A. Graul
Technical Director: Rita C. Opseth
Project Manager: Linda S. Halls
Senior Art Director: Lisa Rosenthal
Art Director: Delores Swanson
Writer: Rita C. Opseth
Editors: Janice Cauley, Bernice Maehren
Sample Coordinator: Carol Olson
Technical Photo Director: Bridget
  Haugh
Fabric Editor: Bobbette Destiche,
  Joanne Wawra
Research Assistant: Lori Ritter
Sewing Staff: Ray W. Arndt, Sr., Janell
  Colley, Phyllis Galbraith, Bridget
  Haugh, Sara Holmen, Linda Neubauer,
  Carol Olson, Carol Pilot, Wendy
  Sotebeer, Nancy Sundeen

*Director of Development Planning
  & Production:* Jim Bindas
Photo Studio Manager: Rebecca Boyle
Photographers: Rex Irmen, John
  Lauenstein, Bill Lindner, Mette
  Nielsen, Cathleen Shannon
Lead Photographers: Mark Macemon,
  Mike Parker
Production Manager: Amelia Merz
Electronic Publishing Analyst:
  Kevin D. Frakes
Production Staff: Joe Fahey, Peter
  Gloege, Melissa Grabanski, Mark
  Jacobson, Daniel Meyers, Linda
  Schloegel, Nik Wogstad
Prop & Rigging Supervisor: Greg Wallace
Prop Stylist: Jim Huntley
Consultants: Ray W. Arndt, Sr., Barbara
  Blank, Stephanie Carter, Paul Currie,
  Joyce Eide, Kathy Ellingson, Amy
  Engman, Wendy Fedie, Chris Hansen,
  Sara Holmen, Joan Maus, Susan Mullins,
  Linda Neubauer, Diane Schultz, Dorothy
  Collins Shepherd, Nancy Sundeen,
  Donna Whitman
Contributors: Andersen Windows,
  Inc.; Calico Corners Decorative
  Fabrics; Coats & Clark Inc.; Conso
  Products Company; Creative Home
  Textiles/Mill Creek; Dyno Merchandise
  Corp.; Graber Industries, Inc.;
  Keith Raivo Designs; Kirsch; Laces &
  Lacemaking; Land o' Lace; Scandia
  Down Shops; The Singer Company;

Spartex Inc.; Swiss-Metrosene, Inc.;
Waverly, Division of F. Schumacher &
Company; Windmill Imports, Inc.
Printed on American paper by: Ringier
America, Inc. (0992)

Cy DeCosse Incorporated offers
craft and sewing accessories to
subscribers. For information write:
  Craft Accessories
  5900 Green Oak Drive
  Minnetonka, MN 55343